Women Writers

JANE AUSTEN

Meenakshi Mukherjee

First published 1991

Published by
MACMILLAN EDUCATION LTD
Houndmills, Basingstoke, Hampshire RG21 2XS
and London
Companies and representatives
throughout the world

Typeset by BP Integraphics, Bath, Avon

Printed in Hong Kong

British Library Cataloguing in Publication Data
Mukherjee, Meenakshi
Jane Austen.
1. Fiction in English. Austen, Jane 1775–1817
I. Title
823.7
ISBN 0–333–39262–0 (hc)
ISBN 0–333–39665–0 (pbk)

Contents

Editors' Preface	vii
Acknowledgements	viii
1. 'Gentlemen read better books'	1
2. 'But you know, we must marry'	28
3. 'To hear my uncle talk of the West Indies'	49
4. 'Crowd in a little room'	70
5. 'Admiring Pope no more than is proper'	89
6. 'Speak well enough to be unintelligible'	110
Conclusion	136
Appendix: 'Plan of a Novel, according to hints from various quarters'	143
Notes	147
Bibliography	154
Index	164

Editors' Preface

The study of women's writing has been long neglected by a male critical establishment both in academic circles and beyond. As a result, many women writers have either been unfairly neglected or have been marginalised in some way, so that their true influence and importance has been ignored. Other women writers have been accepted by male critics and academics, but on terms which seem, to many women readers of this generation, to be false or simplistic. In the past the internal conflicts involved in being a woman in a male-dominated society have been largely ignored by readers of both sexes, and this has affected our reading of women's work. The time has come for a serious reassessment of women's writing in the light of what we understand today.

This series is designed to help in that reassessment.

All the books are written by women because we believe that men's understanding of feminist critique is only, at best, partial. And besides, men have held the floor quite long enough.

EVA FIGES
ADELE KING

Acknowledgements

I thank my students and colleagues in the University of Hyderabad and in Jawaharlal Nehru University who have helped me through discussions. I am grateful to my friends Janet Todd, Maria Couto and Harish Trivedi for their help with books and ideas; to Veena and Rita who helped in preparing the typescript; to Sujit Mukherjee, who patiently read the first draft and offered critical comments; and to Rukmini and Shumeet for their assistance during the final revision.

New Delhi   M.M.

1 'Gentlemen read better books'

'But you never read novels, I dare say?'
'Why not?'
'Because they are not clever enough for you;
gentlemen read better books!

Northanger Abbey

... women who are amused by the reveries of
the stupid novelists, who, knowing little of human
nature, work up stale tales and describe meretri-
cious scenes, all retailed in a sentimental jargon,
which equally tend to corrupt the taste and draw
the heart aside from its daily duties.

Mary Wollstonecraft,
Vindication of the Rights of Woman

The last quarter of the eighteenth century, when Jane Austen (1775–1817) was born and grew up, happened to be
a period of unprecedented expansion for the English novel,
in terms both of the number of works produced and of
the rate at which they were consumed, chiefly through
the commercial institution called the circulating library.
Most of the widely read books of the time – about half
of which were written by women – have now been forgotten, but we should bear in mind that Jane Austen, despite
her literary admiration for Richardson, Cowper, Crabbe

1

and Johnson, read the popular books no less avidly – though perhaps more critically – than her heroine Catherine Morland, and wrote her novels under and against the influence of the romantic, gothic and sentimental fiction which flooded the market at the time. It was also a period when the respectability of the novel as a genre was at its lowest ebb. Both moralists and literary purists were alarmed about the harm it was doing to its readers, who were alleged to be predominantly young and female. Many of the fiction-writers at this time were also women, and the tendency to relegate the entire production and consumption process to the feminine domain may have contributed to the low esteem in which the novel was held. The *Monthly* commented in 1773, 'This branch of the literary trade appears now to be almost engrossed by ladies.'[1] The shrill condemnation of novel-reading – from the pulpit, from writers of conduct books and from the lawgivers in literary periodicals – did nothing to curb its popularity, however. Fanny Burney observed in her Preface to *Evelina*, 'Their contagion bids defiance to the medicine of advice of reprehension.' Her choice of the metaphor of disease betrays her uneasy relationship with the genre, which she had herself done much to popularise. Maria Edgeworth, Amelia Opie, Elizabeth Inchbald and other contemporary practitioners of the art of fiction likewise went to great lengths to profess that what they were writing should not be included in that pernicious category of enticement called the 'novel'.

In this context Jane Austen stands out as a very unusual figure. Not only did she confer credibility upon this despised genre, but she also was quite unapologetic about the female orientation of her work and the fact that it did not seek to instruct. Without ruffling the smooth surface of her novels she managed to introduce into them some of the ideological debates of her time which questioned the implied assumptions behind the gender-based codes of conduct. For example, in Elizabeth Bennet's refusal of Mr Collins' marriage proposal and his reaction to it in *Pride and Prejudice*, we witness a comic rendering of an essentially serious confrontation between two ideologies of marriage and two opposing images of women. One of these can be traced back of Rousseau, who had argued that 'woman is framed particularly for the delight and pleasure of man'.[2] By implication, the essence of femininity lay in the application of subtle and arch strategies for attracting men. The other and less popular view, argued by Mary Wollstonecraft among others, granted the same rationality and autonomy to women as to other human beings. Mr Collins cannot believe Elizabeth's rejection of him. He must interpret it as her 'wish of increasing [his] love by suspense according to the usual practice of elegant females' (ch. 19). Elizabeth's exasperated reply, 'Do not consider me now as an elegant female intending to plague you, but as a rational creature speaking the truth directly from her heart', points to a crucial dilemma of the intelligent woman in late-eighteenth-century England, both in fiction and in real life.

All through the eighteenth century, the thinkers and philosophers following John Locke generally stressed the importance of reason in human behaviour. Coming towards the end of the century, Jane Austen must have imbibed this Augustan heritage; but, when it came to the question of women's education and ideals of feminine behaviour, society somehow expected a willing suspension of logic. Each of Jane Austen's six novels presents in some form of the other the deep-seated contradiction between the rational norm in eighteenth-century society and the standards to which women were, hypocritically, expected to adhere.

A romantic and idealised helplessness with its corollary of affectation and pretence were considered to be desirable attributes in women and were propagated by most writers,

men and women alike. The cynical wisdom of the Earl
of Chesterfield, who saw women as 'children of a larger
growth',[3] was recorded in his *Letter to his Son* a year before
Jane Austen was born. This was echoed by Hannah More
in the next decade, when she marshalled arguments to
prove that logic and abstract thought were foreign to
women.[4] While men were constantly being conditioned
by history, influenced and modified by the new ideas of
individualism and empirical pragmatism that led to the
ideal of the self-made man and to the spread of the empire,
women were confined within strict limits, seen as subject
to timeless values. Into this society Jane Austen was born
in 1775, five years after Wordsworth, four years after
Walter Scott and three years after Coleridge. Coleridge
was a vicar's son from Devon, and Jane Austen was born
in a rural rectory at Steventon, Hampshire, but their lives
and world views were to be vastly different: as a daughter
of her family, Jane Austen was destined for a life of
restricted mobility, and subjected to an education and a
moral code calculated to resist the forces of history. Part
of our interest in Jane Austen today lies in her ability to
subvert the limitations imposed on her by society, and to
undermine the values she was supposed to uphold. At one
time she was considered to be an unambiguous writer who
reassured the reader about the order and stability of
society, confirming in the process the norms of patriarchy.
Today we cannot ignore the fact that the apparently placid
texture of her novels conceals a tension between protest
and acceptance, rebellion and conformity, held in equili-
brium by the controlling device of comedy.

Rationality and individualism were the leading concepts
of the age, but neither was seen as particularly relevant
to women, who were not educated to be individuals but
only to fill social and familial slots. The skills that they
were expected to learn were those that would secure them
a husband, who would confer identity and status. The edu-

cation of young women was a major topic of discussion in the eighteenth century, and the books on conduct with practical advice on social skills and moral value did a lot to codify and disseminate ideas about a woman's role in society. The most popular writers of such works – Dr John Gregory, the Reverend James Fordyce, Jane West, Mrs Chapone, Hannah More – blended moral and social advice so skilfully that the approved double standard acquired almost a scriptural and timeless sanction. Hannah More talked of the 'porcelain clay' of which women are made:

> Greater delicacy evidently implies greater fragility: and the weakness, natural and moral, clearly points out the necessity of a superior degree of caution, retirement and reserve . . . They find their protection in their weakness and their safety in their delicacy.[5]

Through a different metaphor Jane West reiterated the same wisdom:

> The perishable commodity of female fame is embarked in a slight felucca . . . [by] no means fitted for those distant voyages and rough encounters with winds, seas and enemies which afford navigators of the other sex a welcome opportunity of showing their skill and magnanimity . . . I cannot therefore think it expedient that these fragile barks should do more than sail *coastwise* till they are taken in tow by some stouter vessel.[6]

Any number of similar exhortations can be culled from the popular conduct books of the time, all of which see woman's weakness as her most attractive feature, and the one that she should play on to captivate a husband. The cult of the frail heroine who faints and swoons is thus closely bound up with this concept of indirect feminine power.

The degree to which women ought to aspire to physical strength was a fairly controversial issue in Jane Austen's time. The liberal thinkers on women's conduct advocated a rational education leading to a strong mind and a strong body alike, which would enable girls to become good Christians and sensible human beings. Tame as this agenda may sound today, it was out of step with the conservative ideology that implicitly linked virtue with physical frailty in women. Novel after novel idealised the fragile heroine who fainted when her virtue was assaulted or pined away when wronged in love. As Claudia Johnson has pointed out, Clarissa's death in Richardson's novel, which was really a 'twisted testimonial to male power', was seen at the time as a triumph of virtue.[7] The plight of Olivia in *The Vicar of Wakefield*, who occasioned that well-known song of dubious morality

> When lovely woman stoops to folly
> And finds too late that men betray
> What charm can soothe her melancholy
> What art can wash her guilt away?
> The only art her guilt to cover,
> To hide her shame from every eye,
> To give repentance to her lover
> And wring his bosom – is to die!
> (*Vicar of Wakefield*, ch. 29)

served to reconfirm the belief that a woman rejected by a man has no reason whatsoever to continue to live.

Janet Todd argues that this physical debility in women became in due course not only an attribute of purity but also a kind of seductiveness:

The feebleness to which the tender frame of woman is subject is perhaps more seducing than her bloom ... in nursing that which *droops* (sweetly dejected) and is

ready to fall upon its bed, our care becomes more dear
... objects are beloved in proportion ... as they are
gentle, unresisting, and pathetic.[8]

Through her creation of several robust and forthright
heroines (Catherine Morland, Elizabeth Bennet, Emma
Woodhouse), her negative representation of affected
women who exploit their weakness to gain power (Isabella
Thorpe, Louisa Musgrove, Miss Bingley), and her privileging of strength and forbearance over febrile helplessness
(Elinor and Marianne Dashwood), Jane Austen contributed to a continuing debate about frailty and cunning
as necessary feminine characteristics and part of woman's
legitimate armoury. The debate goes back perhaps to
Rousseau's book on education, *Emilius*, where he laid
down the essential difference between men and women:
'One must be active and strong, the other passive and feeble; one must necessarily have power and will; it is suffi-
cient that the other makes but a faint resistance...'[9]
Rousseau went on to argue that God compensated woman
for her physical weakness by giving her beauty, subtlety
and cunning to captivate men. Thus cunning or duplicity
was seen to be almost a fundamental right which a woman
ought to use to her best advantage. Most of the conduct-
book writers of the eighteenth century continued implicitly
to accept this, suggesting ways in which a woman might
render herself more alluring in the eyes of men; but in
the last decade of the century at least two dissenting voices
were heard.

The first was that of the historian Catherine Macaulay
Graham, who pleaded for a regular formal education for
women along rational lines, so that 'when the sex has been
taught wisdom by education, they will be glad to give up
indirect influence for rational privileges'.[10] The second was
the voice of Mary Wollstonecraft, whose *Vindication of
the Rights of Woman* (1792) argued that women should

have a proper education so that they would not have to resort to indirect and artful means to gain power over men. Wollstonecraft berated the conduct-book writers for being more anxious to fashion 'alluring mistresses than affectionate wives and rational mothers'. Condemning the devices of cunning and dissimulation that women were taught in these books, she added, 'In a seraglio I grant that all these arts are necessary.'[11]

Despite the popular image of Jane Austen as a conservative, in the debate on women's education and upbringing she repeatedly took a radical stand. The behaviour of Elizabeth Bennet runs counter to most norms laid down by the conduct books. She is independent, unaffected and intelligent; her unabashed walk through the muddy countryside to see her sick sister violates the code of female propriety. Jane Austen's high-spirited mockery of the fashionable affectation of frailty can also be seen in her early fragment *Love and Friendship*, in the dying advice of Sophia to her daughter Laura:

> My beloved Laura ... take warning from my unhappy End & ... beware of fainting fits ... One fatal swoon has cost me my life ... Beware of swoons, Dear Laura ... A frenzy fit is not one quarter so pernicious: it is an exercise to the Body & if not too violent, is, I dare say conducive to Health in its consequences. – Run mad as often as you chuse, but do not faint ...[12]

The rejection of the standard notions of femininity is again evident in the early chapters of *Northanger Abbey*, where the author in mock despair laments that Catherine Morland, who preferred rough boys' games to elegant occupations such as watering a rose-bush or feeding a canary, was quite unsuited to the role of heroine. 'She was moreover noisy and wild, hated confinement and cleanliness, and loved nothing so well in the world as rolling down the green slope at the back of the house' (ch. 1). As if this was not enough, when the man she thinks she is in love with fails to show up at a ball the disappointed Catherine returns home *not* to weep to to toss sleeplessly in bed, but instead to 'appease' her 'extraordinary hunger' and then to fall asleep for nine solid hours. Her physical energy and spontaneity provide a contrast with Isabella Thorpe, the arch and affected husband-hunter, who perfectly fitted the conventional role model of a feminine woman as well as the fictional stereotype of a woman of sensibility.

Jane Austen's rejection of the excessive emotionalism that the cult of sensibility made fashionable was not so much a reactionary stand in favour of Augustan orthodoxy and against the tide of romantic extravagance as a complex political stand in favour of female autonomy. Similar contrasts, between vitality and sense on the one hand and debility and sentiment on the other, appear, though less emphatically, in *Pride and Prejudice* (between Elizabeth Bennet and Miss Bingley), *Persuasion* (between Anne Elliot and Louisa Musgrove) and *Sense and Sensibility* (between Elinor Dashwood and Lucy Steele).

Elizabeth reads a book when she wants to; Miss Bingley reads to win Darcy's approval. She pretends to dislike dancing only because Darcy is known to dislike it, and walks up and down a room only to show her figure to advantage. Elizabeth, on the other hand, stands out as a self-sufficient person who does not need a man's attention to prove her worth to herself. Like Emma Woodhouse and Catherine Morland, two of Jane Austen's other lively heroines, she is a complete individual, not waiting for a man to give her completion and identity. Also, all three of them are women of remarkable health, fond of the open air and outdoor walks, unlike their fragile predecessors – Richardson's Pamela or Goldsmith's Olivia – who displayed marked tendencies towards fainting. The fact that a frail body in women came to be associated with delicacy

and refinement – at least in fiction – may also be an indirect
outcome of the middle-class aspiration for the leisured life-
style of the upper class. What Ian Watt calls 'sociosomatic
snobbery' enables Pamela to take on the physical symptoms of the women above her class when her humble birth
ought to have made her more sturdy. Although the question of class distinction is not a central issue in Jane Austen
– partly because most of her characters belong to roughly
the same class – she was familiar with the fictional ethos
where 'a conspicuously weak constitution was both an
assertion of a delicately nurtured past and a presumptive
claim to a similar future'.[13] Jane Austen's novels are particularly striking for their refusal to eroticise female inani-
tion and to promote the cult of vulnerability.

Jane Austen was not the only one to insist on strength,
rationality and autonomy in women. In a much more tenta-
tive way Fanny Burney had earlier created such a contrast
in *Evelina* (1778) – between Mrs Selwyn the cynical wit
and Lady Louisa the self-styled 'sad weak creature' – but
with characteristic ambivalence she kept her heroine safely
outside any controversy, making her dependent and vulnerable and thus conventionally feminine. Outside fiction,
however, in the realm of ideas, there was a growing awareness of woman's rights and women's need for rational education. This culminated in the 1790s in the works of
Catherine Macaulay Graham and the much-discussed trea-
tises by Mary Wollstonecraft. Arguing that women needed
balanced physical and intellectual training as much as men
did, Catherine Macaulay Graham declared that until
women enjoyed such an education 'my sex will continue
to lisp with their tongues, to totter in their walk and to
counterfeit more weakness and sickness than they really
have, in order to attract the notice of the male'.[14]

Wollstonecraft devoted nearly two hundred pages of the
Vindication to her case for giving women an education that
would make them physically and emotionally independent:

'the woman who strengthens her body and exercises her mind will, by managing her family and practising various virtues, become the friend, and not the humble dependent of her husband'.[15] Yet the entire movement came to be discredited within a decade through certain accidental circumstances, and by the beginning of the nineteenth century an opposite reaction had set in. When Catherine Macaulay Graham, who had a considerable reputation as a historian, took as her second husband a man much younger then herself, her public image was considerably tarnished, and her opinions about women's education became devalued in the public mind. What happened to Mary Wollstonecraft's reputation after her death is a fairly well-known story. Her husband, William Godwin, wrote an honest account of her unorthodox life, meant as a tribute to Mary's memory, but this scandalised the public. The unconventionalities in her personal life were seen as evidence of the immorality of the whole women's rights movement, and women writers such as Elizabeth Inchbald and Amelia Opie, who had been friends of Mary and had shared some of her views, retreated into conservatism. Hannah More, who always had orthodox views on the matter, now became almost hysterical, and wrote a book castigating Mary's character and vilifying her ideas.[16] It was only natural that in this charged and emotional atmosphere women who might privately have held moderately radical and progressive views should have refrained from expressing them openly, for fear of the social consequences. When, after Jane Austen's death, her letters were published, and biographies of her by her brother Henry Thomas Austen (1818) and her nephew J. E. Austen-Leigh (1871)[17] appeared, the family attempted to suppress all remarks and ideas that could remotely be construed as feminist so that she could remain uncontaminated by controversy. J. E. Austen-Leigh makes sure to inform us that his aunt's 'needlework, both plain and ornamental, was excellent, and might have put a sewing machine to shame. She was considered especially great in Satin stitch'. She 'was fond of music, and had a sweet voice, both in singing and in conversation' and 'Christian love and humility abounded in her heart'.[18] The impression thus created that Jane Austen's moral values and her view of the woman's place in society were uncritically orthodox persisted for a long time.

Although there can be few serious critics of the English novel who have not written on Jane Austen, until the 1980's she had seldom been considered from the perspective of her situation in life as a woman and her views on women's place in society. The reasons for this omission are several. The early enthusiasts made so much of the safe and innocuous maiden-aunt image and her miniature ivory work of domestic patterns that mid-twentieth-century critics such as Mary Lascelles, Marvin Mudrick and D. W. Harding, while analysing her ironic vision and moral concerns, tended to shy away from the fact of her femininity. When she was placed at the head of the Great Tradition in 1948, she was granted, as it were, honorary male status, and her contribution to the English novel assessed without regard to her sex. Feminist criticism was virtually unknown at that time, and, even when women critics such as Barbara Hardy and Marilyn Butler published perceptive studies of Jane Austen's work, they too preferred not to emphasise her femaleness. The general belief that Jane Austen unquestioningly accepted patriarchal values alienated her from the majority of the serious feminist critics who came into prominence in the 1970s on both sides of the Atlantic.

The climate of critical opinion changed considerably in the 1980s after the publication of the influential book by Sandra Gilbert and Susan Gubar, *The Madwoman in the Attic* (1979). The journal *Woman and Literature (formerly Mary Wollstonecraft Newsletter)* brought out a special issue on Jane Austen in 1982 (edited by Janet Todd), and in 1983 Margaret Kirkham's *Jane Austen: Feminism and Fic-*

tion placed her right in the mainstream of the intellectual tradition of Enlightenment feminism that began in the late seventeenth and early eighteenth centuries with Mary Astell and continued until after the French Revolution, culminating in the works of Mary Wollstonecraft.

An interesting reflection of this gradual change can be seen in the way critics have perceived Jane Austen's attitude to Mary Wollstonecraft and her ideas. In 1929 Virginia Woolf had talked of 'glaring discords among intelligent people' such as Jane Austen and Mary Wollstonecraft, and explained the difference in terms of personal experience and family circumstances.[19] In 1966 Frank Bradbrook claimed in his account *Jane Austen and her Predecessors* that Wollstonecraft's feminism was 'extreme' and Jane Austen 'despised' it accordingly. In 1973 Lloyd Brown began to doubt if Jane Austen really despised the writer of *Vindication of the Rights of Woman*. He noted that 'There is no documentary evidence for the belief' and argued that, in view of the many resemblances in their ideas, it was perverse to assume that Jane Austen disliked Mary Wollstonecraft merely because she did not refer to her by name.[20] In 1983 we were offered a reason why she was not referred to by name. Margaret Kirkham argued, with some evidence and a great deal of persuasive logic,[21] that Jane Austen supported many of Wollstonecraft's opinions, including her criticism of Rousseau's view of women's education and his romantic idealisation of a woman at the cost of her rationality. But Godwin's publication in 1798 of his *Memoirs* of his wife had such severe moral repercussions that Jane Austen probably had to avoid aligning with her controversial predecessor. In fact this scandal set back the feminist cause by more than a generation.

Although Jane Austen lived in the pastoral south of England, wrote about the politically untroubled lives of the leisured gentry, and had little personal contact with the turbulent intellectual and literary life of London in the decade following the French Revolution, she was an avid reader: at nineteen she was a pre-publication subscriber to Fanny Burney's *Camilla*, and her letters mention numerous novels and a wide range of other works, including sermons, poetry, biography and history.[22] It is therefore unlikely that she was ignorant of the work of contemporary women writers such as Charlotte Smith, Amelia Opie, Elizabeth Inchbald and Mary Wollstonecraft, most of whom knew each other and in a loose way belonged to the same circle in London. The lives of some of these writers were curiously entangled: William Godwin (1756–1836) is said to have proposed to Amelia Alderson (1769–1836: she later married the painter John Opie) before he started living with Mary Wollstonecraft; Amelia herself was an ardent fan of Mary's writing and wrote her many letters before actually meeting her; there were rumours at one point that John Opie and Mary were to be married. In a letter written to Mary in 1796 Amelia referred to this rumour and commented that, while she could quite believe that Opie should want to marry Mary, she could not believe that Mary was disposed to accept. It seems that Opie remained on friendly terms with Mary, because he painted her portrait after her marriage with Godwin, but the friendship of the two women did not survive Mary's marriage.

In 1800, after Mary died, Amelia Opie wrote a novel, *Father and Daughter*, in which the predicament of the central character bears some similarity to Mary Wollstonecraft's situation in real life. The heroine has an illegitimate child and, after being deceived by her lover, tries to make a living by running a school. In spite of her sympathy for the heroine, Amelia Opie cannot quite condone her moral lapse and makes her die at the end, almost as a punishment. Moreover, her changed attitude to her one-time idol is evident in the long peroration at the end of the novel about the moral attitudes of some writers, which obviously is targeted at Mary Wollstonecraft's *Wrongs of Woman*. Amelia Opie laments how it had become the fashion 'to inveigh bitterly against society for excluding from its circle. . .the woman who has once transgressed the salutary laws of Chastity'.[23] In her view such arguments are fraught with mischief, as they are calculated to 'deter the victim of seduction from penitence': 'But it is not to be expected that society should open its arms to receive its prodigal children till they have undergone a long and painful probation.'[24] We have no direct knowledge about Jane Austen's views on Mary Wollstonecraft's *Wrongs of Woman*, but indirect parodic digs at the moral assumptions behind Amelia Opie's *Father and Daughter* can be seen in the playful 'Plan of a Novel' that Jane Austen wrote towards the end of her life (see Appendix).

Another writer of this circle, Elizabeth Inchbald (1753–1821), was an actress, a playwright and the author of a very popular novel, *A Simple Story* (1790). An attractive woman, she had a wide range of friends, including William Godwin, Thomas Holcroft and other Jacobin writers. Coleridge is said to have remarked that he would run away through the world's wilderness to avoid her 'heart-picking look'. Either in jest or jealousy, Mary Wollstonecraft called her 'Miss Perfection'. Inchbald dropped Mary and Godwin from her circle of friends after they were married, as she was unwilling to 'compromise' herself by being seen in Mary's company. In her writing too one notices a gradual shift towards orthodoxy on the question of woman's place in society. In her earlier plays such as *Everyone Has His Fault* (1793), she took an ambiguous stance, half with and half against the writer of *Vindication of the Rights of Woman*. In the Prologue to the play she wrote,

> *The Rights of Woman* says a female pen
> Are to do everything as well as Men.

> To think, to argue, to decide, to write,
> To talk undoubtedly – perhaps to fight.
>   . . .
> I grant that nature and their frailty such
> Women may make too free – and know too much,
> But since the sex at length has been inclined
> To cultivate that useful part – the mind;
> Since they have learnt to read, to write, to spell,
> Since some of them have wit – and use it well;
> Let us not force them back with brow severe
> Within the pale of ignorance and fear
> Confined entirely to domestic arts
> Producing only children, pies and tarts. . . .[25]

From this qualified and cautious pleading of the feminist cause she shifted to the totally reactionary stand of *Wives as They Were and Maids as They Are* (1797). This later play attempts to prove that the best marriage is one in which the husband is the unquestioned master. In the last scene Lord Priory locks up his wife and makes her do all the domestic work, with the full approval of the playwright. One is tempted to attribute this increased orthodoxy to the opprobrium in which feminist discourse came to be held towards the end of the century, when arguments for women's rights were beginning to be branded as arguments for promiscuity. In a language of unsurpassed hatred and intensity, another contemporary, Hannah More, directly charged Mary Wollstonecraft with promoting immoral practices:

> a direct vindication of adultery was for the first time attempted by a *Woman*, a professed admirer and imitator of the German suicide Werter. The *female* Werter as she is styled by her biographer, asserts in a work entitled 'The Wrongs of Woman' that adultery is justifiable, and that the restrictions placed on it by the laws of England constitute one of the *Wrongs of Woman* . . .

This cool calculating intellectual wickedness eats at the very heart of and core of virtue, and like a deadly mildew blights and shrivels the blooming promise of human spring.[26]

The virulence of Hannah More's rhetoric is an indication of the force of public opinion on such matters. Following her death Mary Wollstonecraft's life turned into a dark legend: seldom does one find one woman figuring in so many books either in her own person or in a fictional guise. It has been pointed out recently that Elinor in Fanny Burney's *The Wanderer* (1814) may well be a late reincarnation of this legend.[27] The contradiction between Mary's emphasis on reason in her discursive writing and the impulsive acts of her own life, including two attempts at suicide, is re-created in the character of Elinor, a militant champion of woman's freedom who is not treated sympathetically by Fanny Burney. Similarly, when Jane West, in her *Letters to a Young Lady*, recommends that women should be unreflective and free from any 'affection of superior knowledge', she cannot resist a sideways swipe at Mary Wollstonecraft, who had challenged this feminine ideal: 'Unengaging as this character (a conventional woman) is, I confess that I greatly prefer it to the petticoat philosophists, who seek for eminence and distinction in infidelity and scepticism, or in the equally monstrous extravagances of German morality.'[28]

Jane Austen was twenty-two when Mary died, and it seems unlikely that she was ignorant of the intellectual and moral ferment that Mary's life and ideas had caused. It is significant that, unlike most other women writers of the time, who directly or indirectly attacked her, Jane Austen maintained total silence on the subject of Mary Wollstonecraft. Only in certain turns of phrase – such as Mrs Croft's protest to her brother, 'But I hate to hear you talk so like a fine gentleman ... as if women were all fine

ladies, instead of rational creatures' (*Persuasion*, ch. 8),
or Elizabeth Bennet's exasperated reply to Mr Collins,
'Do not consider me now as an elegant female, intending
to plague you, but as a rational creature' (*Pride and Prejudice*, ch. 19) – do we find suggestions of an alignment that
cannot be substantiated with more concrete textual evidence.

If in certain places Jane Austen's assumptions and
attitudes come very close to Mary Wollstonecraft's pro-
fessed ideas, it is difficult to determine whether the younger
woman was influenced by the older or whether they were
both spontaneously reacting to social practices that restricted a woman's potential as an individual. Wollstonecraft wrote in the *Vindication*, 'What can be more
indelicate than a girl's *coming out* in the fashionable world?
Which in other words, is to bring to a market a marriageable miss, whose person is taken from one public place
to another richly caparisoned'.[29] Edmund Bertram's baf-
flement about the 'ins and outs' of women in *Mansfield
Park* may not be an echo of this but another rational human
being's natural reaction to a social ritual which humiliated
a girl by reducing her to a marketable commodity.[30] Elizabeth Bennet, another sensible and forthright Jane Austen
character, bristles when Lady Catherine asks her how
many of her sisters are 'out'. She also reacts adversely
to her questions about the feminine accomplishments that
Elizabeth and her sisters have acquired: 'Do you play and
sing, Miss Bennet? ... Do your sisters play and sing? ...
Do you draw?' (*Pride and Prejudice*, ch. 29.) It is these
accomplishments that qualified a girl for the marriage market. The entire debate about women's education in the
eighteenth century hinged upon the question of whether
that education should make the woman a better individual
or merely a pleasing companion for man in his moments
of leisure. Most of the conduct-book writers emphasised
the need to teach girls embroidery, a little painting, how

to tinkle away pleasantly at the piano, and other drawing-room arts. Almost all of them warned against excessive reading and advised girls 'to carefully conceal in their conversation any knowledge or learning that they may happen to possess',[31] although at least one of them felt such caution was actually unnecessary. However much a woman might read, 'she will, generally speaking, be found to have less of what is called learning than a common school boy because the female mind in general does not appear capable of attaining too high a degree of perfection in the areas of abstract knowledge'.[32]

A conversation in *Pride and Prejudice* brings out Jane Austen's attitude towards these ideas of standardised social finish for women. Mr Bingley, who knows only women of a certain kind, expresses his amazement at the patience of young ladies, all of whom manage to 'paint tables, cover skreens, net purses' and thereby join the ranks of accomplished women. To his list of feminine skills his sister earnestly adds a few more: 'a thorough knowledge of music, singing, drawing, dancing and the modern languages', not to speak of 'a certain something in her air and manner of walking' (ch. 8). Darcy, on the other hand, demands in a woman more than these decorative graces. He declares that without extensive reading no woman can be called truly accomplished. Elizabeth, who earlier in the evening has been the butt of Miss Bingley's sarcasm for preferring books to a card game, is quick to protest at this impossibly high expectation: 'I never saw such a woman. I never saw such capacity and taste and application and elegance as you describe united.' Elizabeth, whose responses are always direct and spontaneous, could be reacting here to the essential contradiction between the decorative drawing-room arts, which were acquired for public display, and reading, which is a private and intellectual occupation, and to Darcy's unreasonable demand that the two should be combined.

A crucial issue in the eighteenth-century discourse on women's education was what women should read. That women ought to do some reading was agreed by all, and even that custodian of orthodoxy Mrs Hannah More, drew up a list of reading-material which would be safe and was guaranteed not to make women into 'scholastic ladies or female dialecticians'. 'Neither is there any fear that this sort of reading will convert ladies into authors.'[33] Novel-reading was strictly forbidden for presenting precisely this danger. Since the novel lacked an established tradition as a literary genre, and could be written without the advantage of classical learning or intellectual rigour, it was considered to be an easy form of writing at which anyone could have a go. In fact, judging by the number of women who attempted to write fiction in the eighteenth century, it seems that many women readers of fiction were indeed tempted to try their hands at this malleable new kind of writing. But the image of a woman writer challenged the traditional feminine ideal of passivity. As for the reading of novels, no figure of authority, either male or female, and no writer of conduct books encouraged it, though Wollstonecraft grudgingly admitted that 'any kind of reading I think better than leaving a blank still a blank'.[34] Lady Sarah Pennington in *An Unfortunate Mother's Advice to her Absent Daughters* (1761) in principle admitted that some novels 'perhaps do contain a few good morals, but they are not worth the finding where so much rubbish is mixed'.[35] Richardson's Pamela after her elevation to wife-hood and social superiority turns into a hostile critic of the very genre that gave her existence. Novels gave her no pleasure, she pontificates, 'for either they dealt so much in the *Marvellous* and the *improbable* or were . . . *inflaming* to *passions*' (*Pamela*, vol. II, letter 102).

As the novel increased in popularity over the course of the eighteenth century, so moral and aesthetic disapproval of the genre grew in proportion. In part this was a continuation of the puritanical distaste for romances. In 1744, before the term 'novel' became current, Edward Moore in *Fables for the Female Sex* came close to equating the reading of romances with sloth and gin-drinking.[36] There was a fear too, that the emphasis in fiction on people's feelings and passions would disrupt the stability of the social order. Richardson's Pamela felt it her duty to oppose

> the dangerous notion which they [novels] hardly ever fail to propagate, of a *first-sight* love. For there is such a susceptibility supposed on both sides (which however it may pass in a man, very little becomes the female delicacy) that they are smitten with a glance: the fictitious blind god is made a *real* divinity: and too often prudence and discretion are the first offerings at his shrine.
>
> (*Pamela*, vol. II, letter 102)

One of the characters in Hannah More's *Coeleb in Search of Wife* (1808) laments that

> novels, with a very few admirable exceptions, had done infinite mischief, by so completely establishing the omnipotence of love that the young reader was almost systematically taught an unresisting submission to a feeling, because the feeling was commonly represented as irresistible.[37]

This fear was more acute when the reader was a woman who was being specially trained to be submissive. This surrender to feeling was a self-indulgence contrary to the rigorous discipline advocated in contemporary sermons and conduct books. The 'Protestant ethic' which Watt finds inscribed in the early English novel is 'an ethic of denial, restraint, deferred gratification', observes Terry Lovell,[38] and the popular fiction of the time violated some of these

qualities in its emotional extravagance. As the century
wore on and the question of women's education and place
in society gathered momentum, the detractors of novels
also became very shrill:

> Novels which chiefly used to be dangerous in one
> respect, are now become mischievous in a thousand . . .
> Sometimes they concentrate their force and are at once
> employed to diffuse destructive politics, deplorable pro-
> fligacy and impudent infidelity.[39]

The reference obviously was to the radical political and
feminist thought in the works of the Jacobin writers of
the French Revolutionary period, including the two novels
by Mary Wollstonecraft, which were considered particularly subversive.

A different sort of objection to the reading and writing
of novels was that it was a frivolous pastime, demanding
no intellectual rigour or classical learning. Funny Burney
at the age of fifteen burnt an almost fully written novel
partly because writing was a secret indulgence of which
she was ashamed, and partly because she was impressed
with 'ideas that fastened degradation to this class of composition'.[40] The doubts felt about the value of the new genre
were clearly articulated by Clara Reeve, the author of *The
Progress of Romance* (1785):

> Who are they that read novels? . . . not men of learning,
> for they despise them, not men of business, for they
> have other amusements. The middling rank of people
> are the chief if not the only readers, but particularly
> the young, the volatile, the hearts most susceptible to
> impressions.[41]

What Jane Austen felt about contemporary disapproval
of novels is encoded in the reading-habits she ascribes to
her fictional characters. In *Pride and Prejudice*, Mr Collins,

when invited to read to the ladies of the Bennet household, refuses the first book that is offered: 'he started back, and begging pardon protested that he never read novels' (ch. 5). The book he chooses is a well-known conduct-book of the time – *Sermons to Young Women* by the Reverend James Fordyce – which he felt might improve the minds of the Bennet girls. (In Sheridan's *The Rivals*, this is the book that the heroine places on view on her dressing-table when she has pushed her torrid romances out of sight.) In her unfinished novel *Sanditon* Austen presents another comic character who self-righteously condemns novels: 'the mere trash of the common circulating library I hold in the highest contempt', says Sir Edward (ch. 7). John Thorpe in *Northanger Abbey*, a callow braggart, declares with equal indignation, 'I never read novels, I have something else to do' (ch. 7) and ridicules Fanny Burney without having read her. On the other hand, most of Jane Austen's heroines and other positive characters seem to be avid readers. Catherine Morland, initially apologetic about her taste for novels, is pleasantly surprised that an educated man such as Henry Tilney should share her enthusiasm.

Novelists themselves often had an ambivalent attitude towards their own work and insisted that what they were writing were not novels at all but some other species of writing. Maria Edgeworth, an older contemporary of Jane Austen, preferred to call her book *Belinda* (1801) 'A Moral Tale' and not a novel, because 'so much folly, error and vice are disseminated in books classed under this denomination'.[42] Amelia Opie ingeniously attempted to dissociate herself from the disreputable genre by claiming, in the Introduction to her novel *Father and Daughter*, that she had no talent for the complex art of novel writing:

I therefore beg leave to say in the justice to myself that I know 'The Father and Daughter' is wholly devoid of those attempts at strong character, comic situations,

bustle and variety of incident which constitute a NOVEL
and that its highest pretensions are to be a SIMPLE MORAL
TALE.[43]

The insistence on the word 'moral' to describe these narratives was an attempt to detach them from a genre that
was supposed to corrupt the values of its readers. Even
Fanny Burney, whose early novel *Evelina* (1778) was a
runaway success, called her second book a 'work' rather
than a 'novel' to emphasise its edifying character.[44] Elizabeth Inchbald's *A Simple Story* (1791) ends with a gratui-
tous moral about 'the pernicious effects of improper
education' which has little to do with her theme.

Jane Austen's double-edged defence of the novel in
chapter 5 of *Northanger Abbey* is provoked by attitudes
such as these. In this rare authorial intrusion she demands
a better deal for the novel as a genre and attacks hypocritical people who secretly read what they publicly condemn.
But in the same novel she is also able to establish a parodic
or ironic relationship with a literary tradition she professes
to admire. William Empson's statement 'The fundamental
impulse of irony is to score off both the arguments that
have been puzzling you, both sets of sympathies in your
mind'[45] is perfectly illustrated by *Northanger Abbey*, where
a skilful comic balance is maintained between enthusiastic
support for the new genre and an awareness of its sentimental excesses. Jane Austen praises the novel's delineation
of the varieties of human nature, its humour, the concrete-
ness of its language and its realism. To defend the genre
merely on artistic grounds, and within the parameters of
its own identity, without invoking any other sanction –
moral or educational – was certainly a courageous act at
the time.

Jane Austen was an ardent but critical reader of novels.
Her amusement at the more extravagant and formulaic
elements in popular fiction can be seen in her playful 'Plan

of a Novel' (see Appendix). In this parodic compilation she took up well-wishers' suggestions for ways of improving her work – mostly through means that she had scrupulously avoided in all her six novels. The heroine was to be

> a faultless character … perfectly good, with much tenderness & sentiment, & not the least wit – very highly accomplished, understanding modern Languages & (generally speaking) everything that the most accomplished young Women learn, but particularly excelling in Music – her favourite pursuit – and playing equally well on the Piano Forte & Harp – & singing in the first stile.

Tension between love and filial duty was, as J. M. S. Tomkins has pointed out, a major recurring theme in the popular novels towards the end of the eighteenth century: for instance, in Amelia Opie's *Father and Daughter* – a novel that follows some of the basic patterns that Jane Austen mocks in the 'Plan' – the heroine runs away with a suitor of whom her father disapproves and realises her mistake only too late, Jane Austen's proposed heroine was to be perfectly free of this fault: 'she receives repeated offers of marriage – which she always refers wholly to her her Father, exceedingly angry that *he* should not be first applied to'.

The 'Plan' contains indirect references to may other bestselling novels of the time. The hero who would ultimately marry the heroine would first be 'prevented from paying his addresses to her, by some excess of refinement' (as in Charlotte Smith's *Darcy* and Elizabeth Inchbald's *A Simple Story*), and 'Some totally unprincipled & heart-less young Man, desperately in love with the Heroine, & pursuing her with unrelenting passion' would constantly encroach upon her privacy (as in Fanny Burney's *Evelina*). Jane Austen also parodies, with unerring precision and extravagant comic abandon, the gothic novels with their exotic settings, the picaresque narratives with their constant movement, and the novels of sentiment with their melting passion. The heroine and her father are driven from one country of Europe to another by the wicked machinations of the villain until

> they are compelled to retreat into Kamschaka, where the poor Father, quite worn down, finding his end approaching, throws himself on the Ground & after 4 or 5 hours of tender advice & parental Admonition to his miserable Child, expires in a fine burst of Literary Enthusiasm . . .

The different elements in the 'Plan' serve as an inventory of the familiar and recurrent motifs in the popular fiction of the time, testifying to Jane Austen's sharply critical relationship with the contemporary literary scene. It is no mere accident that there is no abandoned daughter in Jane Austen's novels, no orphan with unknown parentage (in *Emma* the discovery of Harriet Smith's parentage is such an anticlimax that it subverts the convention rather than subscribes to it), no romantic young lord, no daughter living in the same house who is forbidden to come before her father, no sentimental father–daughter attachment, no mysterious death and no dramatic recognition scene. The compact neatness of her novels belies the shrewd critical mind that delighted in sifting the available narrative conventions while manipulating some to her own advantage.

Our interest in Jane Austen today lies not just in her crypto-feminism, but also in the way her work responds to two opposite sets of impulses. The two decades during which she wrote most of her work (1798–1818) were a transitional period in English literature, in which the eighteenth-century concern with the social context of human beings gave way to the romantic emphasis on the isolated or the alienated individual. The romantic 'self', we now recognise, was all-male, and the woman could only be seen as the 'other'. Jane Austen takes the woman as individual and places her in a social setting, faced with a choice that is private and personal. A recurrent theme of her novels is the heroine's resistance to the efforts of the patriarchal community to force her into a social role at the cost of her own identity. Similarly, in terms of narrative mode and structure, her work takes elements of the conventional novel and quietly subverts them, without revealing any crack on the surface.

2 'But you know, we must marry'

There is no happiness in love, except at the end of an English Novel.

Anthony Trollope, *Barchester Towers*

... but you know, we must marry. I could do very well single on my part. – A little company, a pleasant ball now and then would be enough for me, if one could be young for ever. But my father cannot provide for us, and it is very bad to grow old and be poor and laughed at.

The Watsons

Every reader of fiction recognises, or unconsciously accepts, that a narrative is both a representation of life and a constructed literary artefact. Even a professedly realistic novel does not escape the current code by which the unorganised events of life are required to be sieved and processed in order to produce an acceptable novel. The two epigraphs to this chapter indicate the opposite poles between which a novelist has to function: the formulaic expectation of a romantic mode and the material conditions that affect human motivation in real life. The more interesting novelists usually get their desired effect in the play between the often intransigent circumstances of the real world and the neat conventions that govern their encoding in fiction. Truth and image modify each other in the process, creating a dynamics of discourse in which the grain of a narrative may not necessarily correspond to the logic of its predetermined closure.

Jane Austen's treatment of marriage – undoubtedly her major theme – illustrates this tension vividly. She is not unique in assigning centrality to marriage in her fiction. It has been a major and recurring concern of the English novel ever since it emerged as a distinct literary form. With the exception of Defoe and Sterne, all the major eighteenth-century novelists tended to write about a web of human relationships out of which at least the central strand terminated in marriage, an event that could serve as a nodal point on which several areas of human experience converged. The particularly British concern with class divisions and the limited opportunities for social mobility, the rich narrative potential of property inheritance, issues of social conformity, parental authority and individual rebellion, economic survival and moral choice, sexual attraction and emotional drama – all these could be subsumed under one central trope, marriage, which became the ritual ending of most novels, and remained so, with death as the other possible alternative, till the end of the nineteenth century. When the central character was a woman, this convention had a special significance. Unlike for men, who could make several choices in their lives and find their place in society through individual enterprise, for women marriage was the only means of social mobility, one of the few areas in which they could exercise choice, and the only means – however illusory – of determining their own identity in a society that denied them any effective autonomy.

As is well known, all six of Jane Austen's novels end with one or more marriages, and thus correspond scrupulously to the framework of fictional convention. Even as representations of life her novels could not have ignored marriage, because in an England where about half the women remained spinsters, marriage was still seen as the aim and prize of a woman's life.[1] For women with no inheritance to fall back on, marriage was a desperate economic need, especially in a society that afforded very little opportunity or sanction for middle-class women to earn a living. The paradox of real life, where those without private income needed marriage most urgently, and those with income were the most sought-after, also provided the dynamics of the plot mechanism necessary in fiction. Among Jane Austen's heroines only Emma Woodhouse with her £30,000 can afford to think of marriage in an uninvolved detached manner, as a game she can play with other people's lives. For most other women, underlying the elegant ritual of love and courtship, and the pleasant routine of balls and picnics and walks, there lurked an unspoken anxiety about the future. The enactment of the ritual was complicated further by the fact that, while a woman's need to get married was much greater than a man's, the pretence had to be kept up that he was the pursuer and she the passive object of pursuit. All the strategies of art and artifice had to be deployed to sustain this myth.

Marriage was certainly a crucial event in the lives of middle-class women, but the ending of each novel with an obligatory marriage was a stylised device to demarcate acceptable areas of fictional discourse. The continuation of these boundaries perpetuated certain myths: for example, that marriage is the single event of significance in a woman's life and that nothing afterwards is of consequence, or that only nubile women can be interesting. Trapped in the specifically male literary constructs of a patriarchal society, women novelists too began to accept these myths as truths universally acknowledged, and seemed implicitly to echo Fanny Burney's arrogant young lord in *Evelina* who says 'I don't know what the devil a woman lives for after thirty. She is only in other folk's way'.[2]

Perhaps it was fortunate for Jane Austen that she preferred to conform to the outer framework of the convention and regard the post-nuptial life of a woman as strictly outside her purview. Her scathing ironic vision of life would have found it difficult to reconcile a description of the heroine's married life with the demands of fiction. Her playful subversion of some of the conventions of the popular novel in *Northanger Abbey* resulted in the non-publication of the manuscript in her lifetime, even though a publisher had paid for it. Ironic interrogation of the hallowed state of matrimony might have proved even more costly to her literary career. Whatever may have been her fictional stand on marriage as a happy ending, one gleans from her letters her misgivings on the subject in real life. She wrote to her favourite niece, Fanny, in 1817, 'Oh what a loss it will be when you are married. You are too agreeable in your single state, too agreeable as a niece: I shall hate you when your delicious play of mind is all settled down into conjugal and maternal affections'.[3]

Although not explicitly stated, and perhaps not consciously intended either, in *Northanger Abbey* the same loss can be perceived in the transformation of the high-spirited Catherine Morland of the early chapters into the subdued and chastened heroine of the concluding pages. The boisterous young girl who 'hated confinement and cleanliness' is changed into a creature inhabiting enclosed space, who reads not romances but moral essays 'appropriate to her silence and sadness' and the wildness of whose imagination has been suitably controlled. Even if we grant that such change is in any case inevitable because adulthood for woman is a fall from freedom, marriage nevertheless intensifies the setting of boundaries and imposition of socially determined roles. The metamorphosis of the impudent and spirited Elizabeth Bennet into a grateful and acquiescent Mrs Darcy evokes a similar sense of disappointment in *Pride and Prejudice*. In *Sense and Sensibility*

Marianne Dashwood's settling-down as Mrs Brandon after marrying the man she had once considered 'old enough to be my father', nearly defeats the convention of happy ending by appearing almost like a punishment for her earlier transgression.

In all fairness one must also admit that none of Jane Austen's heroines is relegated to a marriage of total subservience, and she achieves for them, as far as possible within the given parameters of fictional and social practice, more equal and sensible partnerships than can be seen in the existing marriages in her novels. In fact, the already married couples in her novels display largely the negative possibilities of the conjugal state. There is a splendid array of mismatched couples who cynically accept their fate as the Palmers do in *Sense and Sensibility*:

> His temper might perhaps be a little soured by finding, like many others of his sex, that through some unaccountable bias in favour of beauty, he was the husband of a very silly woman but . . . this kind of blunder was too common for any sensible man to be lastingly hurt by it. (Ch.20)

Elizabeth Bennet's father is another victim of the 'unaccountable bias in favour of beauty'. His realisation of the stupidity of his wife 'had put an end to all real affection for her. Respect, esteem, confidence had vanished forever.' The key words for a happy marriage in Jane Austen turn out to be 'affection', 'respect', 'esteem' and 'confidence', which, with the possible exception of the Gardiners, the Crofts and the Westons, seem to be singularly absent from the domestic sphere of her novels. It is extraordinary that Jane Austen's novels should be so strewn with these uneasy marriages when her main theme is matrimony. The parental figures – the Tilneys, Bennets, Bertrams, Elliots – do not set up any domestic models, and the subsidiary couples (the Allens in *Northanger Abbey*, the Palmers in *Sense and Sensibility*, the Collinses in *Pride and Prejudice*, Charles and Louisa Musgrove in *Persuasion*) hardly make the conjugal state attractive to those about to enter it. The convention of the happy ending therefore is heavily weighed down in Jane Austen's work with the burden of negative examples.

Jane Austen ascribes to her heroines rationality and sense – and sometimes even wit and good humour – to convince the reader about the positive potential of their marriages. But, mercifully, the convention demanded a closure at that point, because there is one consequence of matrimony from which even Jane Austen's ironic mediation could not have protected her heroines if she had to follow their careers after marriage. Although fiction is silent on the messy biological details of life, other evidence of the time tells us of the inexorable cycle of annual pregnancies interrupted by frequent miscarriages that most married women had to go through. In late-eighteenth and early-nineteenth-century England, one child in every four was still-born, and 50 per cent died before they reached the age of two.[4] In a particularly agitated letter which seems to have escaped the vigilance of her relatives who edited them before publication, Jane Austen agonises over yet another pregnancy of a niece who is already overburdened:

> Anna has not a chance of escape. . . . Poor animal, she will be worn out before she is thirty – I am very sorry for her. Mrs Clement too is that way again. I am quite tired of so many children. Mrs Benn has a 13th . . . .[5]

Jane Austen's biographer John Halperin sees in this comment only a spinster's aversion to children and misses her anger at the trapped nature of female existence.[6]

A literary text is made up as much by its thematic designs

as by the gaps and silences that these designs are meant
to conceal. Literature of the time so smoothly glosses over
these disturbing details that the facts that must have been
crucial determinants in a woman's adult life are rendered
virtually invisible. Fictional convention demanded that a
very important aspect of a woman's life should be censored
out of literature. We discover only by chance that Mary
Shelley, who was twenty-two years younger than Jane Austen, had, between the ages of seventeen and twenty-one,
four pregnancies, out of which only one child survived.[7]
She was released from this cycle by Shelley's early death,
but more often it was the woman who succumbed first.
Charlotte Brontë, who was born the year before Jane Austen died, was one of six children born to her mother in
the seven years of her married life. Elizabeth Gaskell in
her biography of Charlotte Brontë casually comments on
the effect of Mrs Brontë's fecundity on her husband, who
'was not naturally fond of children, and felt their frequent
appearance on the scene as a drag both on his wife's
strength and as an interruption to the comfort of the household'.[8] It is disconcerting today to think of the situation
of a woman before she had the means or the power to
control the size of her family. Jane Austen, George Eliot
or even for that matter Virginia Woolf might not have
been the writers they were if they had had to enter this
relentless child-bearing process.

Large families were the norm in Jane Austen's time;
she herself belonged to a family of eight, and in her novels
the Heywoods have fourteen children (*Sanditon*), Catherine Morland's parents ten (*Northanger Abbey*) and the
Prices of Portsmouth at least nine (*Mansfield Park*), while
Emma's sister Isabella has five children in seven years
(*Emma*) and the Musgroves have an unspecified number
of 'boisterous boys' and 'chattering girls' other than the
three elder ones who figure prominently in the novel (*Persuasion*). But this future is not supposed to dampen the

prospect of eternal happiness for the newly-wed couples from whom we part at the end of each novel.

If biology was taboo in fiction, economics was only selectively so. The incomes of prospective heroes could be mentioned and so could the fortunes of the young ladies entering the marriage market – a term that was not, of course, metaphorical. The chances of marriage were subtly calculated on the basis of the portion settled on the girl, a fact that Jane Austen mocks on the first page of *Mansfield Park* by pushing the calculation to an absurd exactitude. Capturing a baronet with only £7000 capital, she informs us, was an unexpected achievement for Maria Ward, who was 'at least three thousand pounds short of any equitable claim to it'. Such accounting was not meant to be done openly and, according to convention, only the villains were supposed to be mercenary. But, when Charlotte Lucas in *Pride and Prejudice* presents her cold-blooded argument in favour of an economic and pragmatic consideration in marriage, she cannot be safely relegated to the category of a villain. We are expected at least to half-sympathise with a woman who, having neither beauty nor money enough to hope for a better establishment, has to settle for the ludicrous Mr Collins. 'I am not a romantic, you know', she tells Elizabeth; 'I ask only a comfortable home' (ch. 22). Similarly ambivalent is Elizabeth Watson's rationalisation in *The Watsons*: 'I do not like marrying a disagreeable man any more than yourself – but I do not think there are very many disagreeable men; – I think I could like any good-humoured man with a comfortable income, (ch. 1). It is true that both Charlotte Lucas and Elizabeth Watson are foils; they make compromises that the heroines will not be expected to make, and are meant to serve a moral purpose by setting expediency against integrity. Yet they are, nevertheless, spared the novelist's total condemnation. Her double-edged vision makes allowance for the fact that some are luckier than others, and achieving a marriage in which romantic fulfilment, social sanction and economic stability are combined – as all six heroines of the finished novels do – is more an idealised fictional device than a commonly obtained condition in life.

Is Jane Austen accepting the convention or undercutting it through parodic strategies? The elusiveness of her ideological stand on marriage, as on other issues, is a perpetual challenge to critics, who have never finally resolved the problem of determining her alignments. The distinction she makes between those who take for granted the manipulative aspect of marriage and those who attempt to resist it seems at first to provide a clear moral divide. In *Sense and Sensibility* the despicable John Dashwood, who is in no way interested in his sisters except as burdens to dispose of, begins calculating as soon as he sees Colonel Brandon:

> 'What is the amount of his fortune?'
> 'I believe about two thousand a year.'
> ... 'Elinor, I wish, with all my heart, it were twice as much, for your sake.'
> 'Indeed I believe you,' replied Elinor,
> 'But I am very sure that Col Brandon has not the smallest wish of marrying me.'
> 'You are mistaken ... A very little trouble on your side secures him. Perhaps just at present he may be undecided; the smallness of your fortune may make him hang back ... There can be no reason why you should not try for him ...'   (ch. 33)

His logic is not very different from that of Charlotte Lucas, who also believes that securing a man is a matter of clever strategy: 'In nine cases out of ten a woman had better show more affection than she feels. When she is secure of him, there will be leisure for falling in love as much as she chuses' (*Pride and Prejudice*, ch. 6). But this borders more on practical wisdom than hypocrisy and we are encouraged to be more critical of John Dashwood than of Charlotte Lucas.

The lacuna in the unspoken law by which the market economy of marriage worked is sardonically laid down in the opening paragraph of *Mansfield Park*: 'But there certainly are not so many men of large fortune in the world as there are pretty women to deserve them.' The equation of money in men and beauty in women is obviously an axiom Jane Austen is exposing to criticism by her literal acceptance of it. Taken to its logical extreme it would legitimise John Dashwood's peevish displeasure at Marianne's illness and consequent loss of her only asset, beauty: 'I question whether Marianne now will marry a man worth more than five or six hundred a year at the utmost' (*Sense and Sensibility*, ch. 33). But beauty is a negotiable and variable factor in this equation and can be compensated for by money. While the woman impoverished by unequal inheritance laws needs financial security in marriage, a man with uncertain assets is willing to settle for a woman with money regardless of her looks. But, while in women the pursuit of financial stability through marriage is to a certain extent accepted as a necessary urge, in men it results in a loss of credibility. Elizabeth Bennet playfully points out this double standard of morality to Mrs Gardiner, who has earlier cautioned her in the name of prudence against marrying Wickham:

Pray, my dear aunt, what is the difference in matrimonial affairs between the mercenary and the prudent motive? Where does discretion end and avarice begin? Last Christmas you were afraid of his marrying me, because it should be imprudent, and now because he is trying to get a girl with one thousand pounds. You want to find out that he is mercenary.

(*Pride and Prejudice*, ch. 27)

In the same novel Captain Fitzwillam handles a similar predicament by honestly admitting his helplessness about money: 'Younger sons cannot marry where they like'. Elizabeth can only counter his confession with wit – her verbal defence in a world in which she is otherwise powerless: 'Unless where they like women of fortune, which I think they often do' (ch. 33).

Willoughby in *Sense and Sensibility* is another self-confessed mercenary, who admits that his love for Marianne, however passionate, is 'insufficient to outweigh that dread of poverty'. In *Sanditon* Sir Edward may think of himself as a dangerously seductive man 'quite in the line of Lovelace', but the world knows better. Lady Denham warns Charlotte by declaring, 'A handsome young fellow like him will go smirking and smiling about and paying girls compliments, but he knows he must marry for money' (ch. 7). This seems to be a socially acceptable position, and Charlotte Smith in her novel *D'Arcy* does not in any way condemn a man who can offer this excuse of not marrying the girl he loves: 'Were I possessed on an independent fortune, she is the only woman who should share it with me, but situated as I am, it cannot be. Of a noble family himself, my father thinks it a duty incumbent on his son, to support its dignity by marriage.'[9]

In Jane Austen, the men who have to pursue prosperity through marriage are sometimes rendered comic or shallow, while women who seem over-anxious in this permitted but supposedly underplayed pursuit are projected as hypocrites (Isabella Thorpe and Lucy Steele, for example). Considering that men and women had to operate within different economic parameters, Jane Austen seems to have let the men off too easily. Women who did not inherit money and were unable to marry money were condemned to a life of destitution, whereas men could go out into the work to seek their fortune – an option that no Jane Austen hero exercises except in her last novel. One of the difficulties that today's reader encounters in reading Jane Austen is the attitude of her characters to money and work, which seems to be partly shared by the author. One gets the impression that, like the blessing of God, the presence or absence of wealth in a man's life is a fact beyond human control. That money is not an immutable quality like intelligence or the colour of one's hair, but an element that responds to individual endeavour, that it can be generated through trade and industry, earned by work and dissipated through bad management, is recognised only in *Persuasion*, her last completed novel. *Sanditon* too contains a somewhat ambiguous awareness of speculative ventures and the dynamic possibilities of England's economy. But till then all her heroes had either inherited wealth (Darcy, Knightley) or a clerical living secured through family patronage or personal favour (Henry Tilney and Edmund Bertram; also Edward Ferrar, who waited endlessly for it to come to him). Only *Persuasion* suggests that the real vitality of the race had passed from the aristocracy and the landed gentry, who inherited wealth, to the professional class, who made it by proving their individual worth at work – in this case, through maritime ventures aimed at securing honour and trade for the country.

In a world where gross material calculations dominated marriage and social intercourse, Jane Austen's heroines are relatively exempt from their effect – Catherine Morland because she is too naïve to understand the code and Marianne Dashwood because she is too impetuous and romantic to comprehend the practical world. But, unlike theirs, Elizabeth Bennet's rejection of material values is a conscious moral stand from where she can counter with scorn Charlotte's well-meaning advice about how to secure a husband: 'Your plan is a good one . . . where nothing is in question, but the desire of being well-married; and if I were determined to get a rich husband, or any husband,

I dare say I should adopt it' (*Pride and Prejudice*, ch. 6).
Her refusal of Darcy's first proposal (like Fanny Price's
rejection of Henry Crawford) is meant to underscore her
private battle against the economic pressures of an acquisitive society. Emma Woodhouse, the inheritor of a comfortable house and a large income, is naturally above
monetary calculations for herself, but, although she is rigid
about class hierarchy, her insensitivity to the economic
basis of bourgeois society, to which she herself belongs,
borders on arrogance. Like the heroine of a later English
novel – Dorothea Booke in *Middlemarch* – Emma's education will not be complete until she has found out 'how
much things cost'. To take the example of yet another
Victorian novel that describes the 'amorous effects of
brass'[10] rather explicitly – *Vanity Fair* (1848) – the counter
pointing of the two heroines, one who understands money
and one who does not, is by no means morally unambiguous. Amelia's ignorance or indifference to money is as
much a moral flaw as Becky's obsession with it. In Jane
Austen, too, money is not necessarily seen as a tainted
substance. Anne Elliot in *Persuasion* knows the value of
money and is capable of effective and detailed management of the household economy of an impoverished father,
yet she has no hesitation in refusing the hand of a future
baronet who would have restored her beloved family mansion to her and guaranteed her affluence for the rest of
her life.

The process of self-definition for a heroine often includes
at least one refusal of a marriage proposal, a plot strategy
that persisted, with interesting variations, up till Henry
James's *Portrait of a Lady* (1880). This can be read as
a symbolic assertion of a woman's will in a society where
the ideology of capitalism sanctioned individual (male)
enterprise in the wider world, but efforts were still being
made to retain the old power structure within the orbit
of the home. Some women writers covertly challenged the

dual values and tried to make the voice of the female individual heard. But as women their heroines were still bereft of political or economic power; the only sphere in which they could exercise a semblance of choice was in the arena of marriage. Even there, as in a country dance which Henry Tilney in *Northanger Abbey* calls an emblem of marriage, only the male could really choose his partner: 'you will allow that in both [a country dance and matrimony] man has the advantage of choice, woman only the power of refusal' (ch. 10).

How often a woman's 'yes' was taken for granted can be seen in *Pride and Prejudice*, where Mr Collins and Darcy, however dissimilar they might be as human beings, are equally surprised by Elizabeth's rejection of their proposals. In *Sense and Sensibility* Elinor is amused at the way a woman's acquiescence is taken for granted:

> 'We think now', said Mr Dashwood ... 'of Robert's marrying Miss Morton'. Elinor, smiling at the grave and decisive importance of her brother's tone, calmly replied:
>
> 'The lady I suppose has no choice in the affair.' ... 'I only mean, that I suppose from your manner of speaking, it must be all the same to Miss Morton whether she marry Edward or Robert.'
>
> 'Certainly, there can be no difference; for Robert will now to all intents, and purposes be considered as the eldest son.' (ch. 41)

Most of Jane Austen's heroines chafe under the burden of feminine passivity, and one of them (Catherine Morland) is ironically reprimanded by the author for having dreamt of a man before he was reported to have dreamt of her. Fanny Price, under collective pressure to accept the proposal of Henry Crawford, protests, 'Let him have all the perfections of the world ... a man [need not] be acceptable to every woman he may happen to like' (*Mansfield Park*, ch. 35) Emma reiterates this declaration of independence: 'A woman is not to marry a man merely because she is asked or because he is attached to her' (*Emma*, ch. 7). Although they appear self-evident today, these assertions of a woman's right to choose needed to be made when her acquiescence was assumed. The assertiveness is extended further in *Persuasion* when in the revised ending Jane Austen lets her heroine take the initiative in eliciting a response from the man. Anne Elliot's avowal of the constancy of a woman's love is overheard by Wentworth, at first perhaps by chance, but she decides to continue her declaration within his hearing and, in effect, confesses her love to him, thus inverting both a literary convention and a social taboo.

In Jane Austen's novels there is a constant tension between a woman's need to exercise choice in order to define herself as an individual and society's demand that she should conform. As a social institution marriage implied subservience and for the imaginative woman it did imply a curtailment. Accepting this as part of God's design, Richardson's conduct-book heroine Pamela makes a maxim out of this situation in the final pages of the book:

> In your *maiden* state, think yourself *above* the gentlemen and they'll think you so too, and address you with reverence and respect ... In your *married* state, which is a kind of state of humiliation for a lady, you must think yourself subordinate to your husband; for so it has pleased God to make the wife.
>
> (*Pamela*, vol. II, letter 103)

But not every fictional heroine had Pamela's total complacency, and, in many subsequent novels where the protagonist is a woman, marriage, while being the desired goal, also triggers off an uneasy sense of anti-climax. Yet no satisfactory alternative was available. In the letter to her niece Fanny in which Jane Austen regretted the prospect of losing a lively niece through marriage, she also added, 'yet I do wish you to marry very much because I know you will never be happy till you are'.

What were the options for the gentlewoman who did not or could not marry, or was widowed without being provided for? In Jane Austen's novels Miss Bates, Mrs Smith and Mrs Norris provide some depressing alternatives. Emma Woodhouse was not afraid of remaining single, because, although a poor old maid was a pitiful creature, 'a single-woman of good fortune is always respectable'. The acquisition of this fortune, however, was a man's affair and a woman could only inherit, not earn, it. Middle-class women had few legitimate ways of becoming self-sufficient through work.

> Though well-bred young women should learn to dance, sing, recite and draw, the end of good education is not that they may become dancers, singers, players or painters; its real object is to make them good daughters, good wives, good mistresses . . . . the above qualifications therefore are intended to *adorn* their leisures, not to employ their lives.[11]

Thus wrote Hannah More in 1778, and in a genteel society the stigma attached to the woman who accepted paid employment continued well into the next century. Hardly any of Jane Austen's women characters do any remunerative work. Mrs Weston in *Emma* used to be the heroine's governess, but by the time the novel begins she has ascended the social ladder to become a gentleman's wife. Jane Fairfax is saved by marriage from the 'governess trade' which might have been her miserable fate. Teaching in a boarding-school and working as a governess were the two dreadful options open to a gentlewoman fallen on evil

days. The exchange between the Watson sisters emphasises
the horror in which the teaching-profession was held. 'I
would rather be a teacher at a school (and I can think
of nothing worse) than marry a man I did not like.' The
spontaneity of Emma Watson's declaration is countered
by her experienced elder sister: 'I would rather do anything
than be a teacher at a school ... *I* have been at school,
Emma, and what a life they lead you; *you* never have'
(*The Watsons*).

The conditions at school in Jane Austen's time must
indeed have been dismal, with serious health hazards com-
pounding other discomforts. Austen's own stint at school
was interrupted when both she and her sister Cassandra
fell ill of the 'putrid' fever, which probably broke out as
an epidemic; the aunt who went to fetch them later died
of the infection.[12] Inevitably this reminds one of Lowood
School in *Jane Eyre*, a cradle of 'fog-bred pestilence',
where 'forty-five out of the eighty girls lay ill at one time'
of typhus fever. It has been shown that this fictional school
corresponded rather closely to Cowan Bridge, the institution where Charlotte Brontë went as a girl; during her
one-year stay, forty girls fell ill during an epidemic of fever
and several died of tuberculosis.[13] If such were the conditions in the 1830s, they could not have been much better
in Jane Austen's time, a generation or two before the
Brontës. It is characteristic of Jane Austen's fictional world
that the only school mentioned is a particularly harmless
one, where 'putrid' fever is not heard of. In Mrs Goodard's
school in *Emma* 'a reasonable quantity of accomplishments
were sold at a reasonable price'; a place 'where girls might
be sent to be out of the way and scramble themselves into
a little education without the danger of coming back prodi-
gies' (ch. 3), it conformed to Hannah More's guidelines.[14]
Although the physical wholesomeness of the school is mentioned, the teachers from this school, except for old Mrs
Goodard, are conspicuously outside Emma's social circle,

even though the Woodhouses are so starved of company. Gentlewomen evidently fell from civilised society once they accepted paid employment.

Mary Wollstonecraft, that extraordinary older contemporary of Jane Austen, tried out nearly all the means of earning money available to gentlewomen of her time. After working as a companion to a rich woman in Bath, she set up her own day-school, a venture that ended in financial loss. Humiliated in her next job as a governess in Ireland, she returned to London determined to make a living by writing, a rare profession for women outside a small liberal circle in London. Jane Austen, who never married, felt the confining effect of a depleted income as she grew older. In her last seven years she devoted herself seriously to writing, but, although success sometimes seemed within reach, in her whole life she never earned more than £700 from her novels. While her publisher paid her £110 for *Pride and Prejudice* in 1812, in 1808 Sir Walter Scott had been offered £1000 for *Marmion* even before the manuscript was submitted, and in 1817 Thomas Moore received £3000 for *Lalla Rookh*.[15]

'Though I like praise as well as anybody, I like what Edward calls Pewter too', she wrote in a letter with characteristic self-mockery.[16] Not much pewter came her way and the reasons cannot now be ascertained with any certainty. Although Crosby, who bought the manuscript of *Northanger Abbey* gave no reason for not publishing it, Margaret Kirkham suggests that he 'suppressed' it for its subversive views on life and literature, its mockery of popular modes of fiction, and the decidedly feminist bias of its defence of the novel in chapter 5.[17] Jane Austen did not deal directly with her publishers. Her father sold the manuscript to Crosby and her brother subsequently negotiated on her behalf, yet the fact that the author was a woman may have distinctly weakened their bargaining position. While it was acceptable for a woman to write

as a hobby, it was considered wrong for her to turn aggres-
sively professional. Dr Johnson's views of 'The Amazon
of the Pen' are well known,[18] and the attitudes remained
much the same even in the next century. When in 1837
Robert Southey wrote that well-known letter to Charlotte
Brontë advising her not to become a writer, he warned
her of two dangers: excessive day dreaming – a pre-con-
dition of writing – might induce a distemper, making her
unfit for the normal female duties; and she might develop
an unhealthy ambition of becoming a celebrity. 'Literature
cannot be the business of a woman's life and it ought not
to be', he admonished her.[19] In an excessively polite and
perhaps slightly ironic reply, Charlotte told him that she
worked as a governess and had hardly any time to day
dream. 'In the evenings I confess I do think ... but I carefully avoid any appearance of preoccupation ... I trust
I shall never more feel ambitious to see my name in print;
if the wish should rise, I'll look at Southey's letter and
suppress it.'[20]

Jane Austen never saw her name in print because during
her lifetime the title-page of her books merely said that
they were 'By a Lady'. Her identity was, however, not
entirely unknown, because in 1815 the Prince Regent suggested through his librarian that her next novel should
be dedicated to him. This patronage did not in any way
alter her economic situation, nor did a review by Scott
(unsigned, though the literary world would have known
the reviewer's identity) improve sales substantially.

A writing career could thus hardly be considered an eco-
nomically viable alternative to marriage, particularly for
a woman of Jane Austen's class, and she was clear-eyed
about it from the beginning. 'Single women have a great
propensity for being poor', she wrote to a niece, and Charlotte Lucas's pronouncement on marriage as 'the only
honourable provision for well-educated young women of
small fortune', which 'however uncertain of giving happi-

ness, must be [the] pleasantest preservative from want', provided a practical summing-up of the situation (*Pride and Prejudice*), ch. 22. It is interesting that none of Jane Austen's characters ever takes up writing, even as a hobby. Perhaps this would have been too radical a departure from the behaviour expected of a heroine. Jane Austen may also have been afraid of obliterating that comic and ironic distance she needed between herself and her created world. It is worth noting that, with the exception of Elizabeth Barrett Browning in *Aurora Leigh*, no nineteenth-century English writer, male or female, created a heroine who writes. The scribbling woman may not have been an attractive feminine image (Henrietta Stackpole in *The Portrait of a Lady* is a case in point), but women writers' avoidance of an experience they knew at first hand may point to deeper anxieties about encroachment upon private space or the vulnerability of their self-image. Mary Poovey points out that 'the very act of a woman writing during a period in which self-assertion was considered "unlady-like" exposes the contradictions inherent in propriety: just as the inhibitions visible in her writing constitute a record of her historical oppression, so the work itself proclaims her momentary, possibly unconscious, but effective defiance'.[21] But this defiance was fraught with ambivalence, and the writer unable or unwilling to distance herself from this experience never attempted to render it in fiction. Jane Austen started writing early, and, judging by her letters, her nieces showed signs of a similar interest, but she blocked the experience out of her fiction and instead gave centrality to a theme that was approved by both social and literary convention: marriage.

As ironic mediations between the available rhetoric of popular fiction and the hard facts of contemporary life, Jane Austen's novels ascribe an importance to marriage that is uneasy and double-edged. The conventional closure is achieved with some abruptness, fore-shortening narrative development. There is an embarrassed avoidance of detail at the climactic moment, as in Darcy's proposal ('He expressed himself on the occasion as sensibly, as warmly as a man violently in love can be supposed to do' – (*Pride and Prejudice*, ch. 58), in Emma's response to Knightley ('what did she say? Just what she ought of course. A lady always does' *Emma*, ch. 49) or the coming together of Edmund and Fanny Price ('exactly at the time when it was quite natural that it should be so, and not a week earlier, Edmund ceased to care about Miss Crawford and became as anxious to marry Fanny as Fanny herself could desire' – *Mansfield Park*, ch. 48). In *Sense and Sensibility* the major event happens off-stage and we are given a brief report:

> How soon he had walked himself into the proper resolution . . . in what manner he expressed himself, and how he was received, need not be particularly told. This only need be said, – that when they all sat down to table at four o' clock . . . he had secured his lady.   (ch. 49)

The dénouement in *Persuasion* is summed up thus: 'Who can be in doubt of what followed? When two young people take it into their heads to marry, they are pretty sure by perseverance to carry this point' (ch. 24). The indirect and hasty reporting of the long-awaited event in each case may testify to the self-consciousness the novelist felt in reconciling the formal demands of the literary construct with her empirical perception of life sharpened by the hard edge of her unflinching ironic vision.

3 'To hear my uncle talk of the West Indies'

'The evenings do not appear long to me, I love to hear my uncle talk of the West Indies. I could listen to him for an hour together.

Mansfield Park

'What a great traveller you must have been, ma'am!' said Mrs Musgrove to Mrs Croft.

'Pretty well, Ma'am, in the fifteen years of my marriage; though many women have done more I have crossed the Atlantic four times, and have been one to the East Indies and back again.'

Persuasion

Even though Jane Austen seems to belong essentially to the green English countryside with neatly trimmed hedgerows before the landscape was sullied by factory smoke, or hybridised by contact with the colonies, it must be recognised that in the late eighteenth century, when Jane Austen was growing up, England's economy was already inextricably tied up with territories overseas. Overt and incidental references to these newly appropriated lands punctuate the literature of the time – fiction and non-fiction alike – permeating sometimes even to the level of metaphors.

In the English imagination at that time the East and the West Indies were invisible sources of wealth, in the pursuit of which one had to suffer some physical privation. In Amelia Opie's sentimental novel *Father and Daughter* this assumption provides the basis of a simile nearly Homeric in its sweep. 'As the adventurer to India while toiling for wealth never loses sight of the hope that he shall spend his fortune in his native land',[1] so Agnes kept up her hope all through her current miseries. Another popular novel, *Darcy* by Charlotte Smith, which contains all the formulaic elements of attempted seduction of a delicate heroine and rescue by a handsome young lord, resolves an impasse in the narrative through news from India. The one obstacle that prevents the heroine from marrying the titled young man is removed when it is discovered that her father too has inherited a title (along with considerable property) from an English nobleman whom he had befriended during his long stay in India: 'He had been settled in the East twelve years, when a gentleman who had possessed a friendship for him from the first of his arrival there, died, leaving his estate and title to Mr. Stuart, with the proviso that the name of Morell should take place of his own'.[2] Both in real life and in fiction young women who were unable to succeed in the matrimonial market at home were often sent off to India to capture wealthy husbands. This became such a cliché of popular romance that the exhuberant young Jane Austen could not suppress a dig at it in one of her early stories subsequently collected in *Juvenilia*. In 'Catherine of the Bower' a reluctant girl was 'obliged to accept the offer of one of her cousins to equip her for the East Indies'. In spite of her lack of enthusiasm for the project this girl managed to acquire a husband 'as soon as she had arrived at Bengal, and she had now been married nearly a twelve month. Splendidly, yet unhappily married.'[3]

Jane Austen was not only writing under and against the

influence of popular fiction: her family circle furnished
real-life examples that reinforced the cliché. Her father's
half-sister Philadelphia travelled to India. The voyage took
eight months, and she subsequently married a surgeon in
Madras, who was a friend of Warren Hastings. Her husband died a month before Jane Austen was born, and the
widowed Mrs Hancock spent most of the next few years
with the Austens at Steventon making India part of Jane
Austen's frame of reference in her childhood. Warren
Hastings' long association with the Austen family has been
remarked on by Jane Austen's biographers.[4] During the
prolonged trial of Hastings for corruption and mismanage-
ment in India (1788–95) the Austens were his staunch
defenders and Jane Austen in her impressionable years
must have heard a great deal about India and Hastings'
career there. Little George Hastings was brought up by
Jane Austen's parents until he died at the age of six. John
Halperin thinks that Jane Austen's cousin Elizabeth Hancock, who visited Steventon several times, may have been
'the illegitimate offspring of Warren Hastings and Philadelphia Hancock'.[5] This extrovert cousin was the chief stimu-
lus behind the family theatricals in the Austen household.
She married the Comte de Fonillide, who was guillotined
in 1794, and in 1797 she married Jane's brother Henry
Austen. 'She was a clever woman, and highly
accomplished, after the French rather than the English
mode; and in those days, when intercourse with the Conti-
nent was long interrupted by war, such an element in the
society of a country parsonage must have been a rare acquisition'.[6]

Thus, unlike the insular Bertram sisters in *Mansfield
Park* and impetuous Marianne Dashwood in *Sense and
Sensibility*, Jane Austen herself was neither unaware of
nor indifferent to the larger world outside England. Of
her two brothers in the Navy, one went to the West Indies
and the Mediterranean, and the other to the East Indies

and China, eventually dying of cholera in Burma at the
age of seventy-four. Thomas Fowle, the young clergyman
engaged to be married to her sister Cassandra, died in
the West Indies, where he had gone as chaplain to a regi-
ment in the hope of an early preferment on his return.[7]
In a letter written by Jane Austen in 1796 there is a playful
and gossipy reference to a Miss Holwell 'who belongs to
the black hole of Calcutta'[8] and was about to marry
someone in the neighbourhood. The Black Hole of Calcutta was the name popularly given to the scene of a supposed atrocity perpetrated on captive British men and
women in 1756 by the Nawab of Bengal. The British officers were under the command of one Holwell, who later
wrote an account of the event. Jane Austen's continued
awareness of India and the other British colonies is con-
firmed by such allusions and by the fact that towards the
end of her life she read a book, borrowed from the circulating library, entitled *Essay on the Military Policy and Institutions of the British Empire* (1810), by Captain Sir Charles
Pasley.[9]

The more intelligent and sensible women in Jane Austen's novels share the author's awareness. In *Sense and
Sensibility* Elinor says of Colonel Brandon, who has served
in the East Indies, 'He has seen a great deal of the world;
has been abroad, has read and has a thinking mind. I have
found him capable of giving me much information on various subjects' (ch. 10). Bur Marianne, impatient of things
unconnected with her immediate interests, dismisses Elinor's remark with a breezy nonchalance: 'That is to say,
he has told you that in the East Indies the climate is hot
and the mosquitoes were troublesome.' Elinor patiently
persists in her defence both of Colonel Brandon and of
her own evaluation of him by pointing out,

'He would have told me so, I doubt not, had I made
any such inquiries, but they happened to be points on

which I had been previously informed.'

'Perhaps,' said Willoughby, 'his observations may have extended to the existence of nabobs, gold mohurs and palanquins.'

It is to be noted that Marianne and Willoughby, the two self-obsessed romantics, seize upon the twin clichés associated with the East – heat and discomfort on the one hand, pomp and splendour on the other – whereas Elinor, like Fanny Price in *Mansfield Park*, is genuinely curious about things and places outside her own experience and immediate concerns.

India figured in the imagination of this period in diverse ways. On the one hand their were the 'nabobs, gold mohurs and palanquins' – stereotypes of the rich and exotic East. On the other hand, India provides a pretext for looking more critically at England's own social system, as in the novels *Translations of the Letters of a Hindoo Rajah* (1796) by Elizabeth Hamilton and *The Empire of the Nairs, an Utopian Romance* by James Lawrence (published in 1811, but written some years earlier). These two popular and now forgotten works of fiction belong to the same tradition at *Utopia* and *Gulliver's Travels*, in which a foreigner's viewpoint or the framework of a travel tale is used to satirise English society. Hamilton's novel uses a rajah's observations to contribute to the debate in England about women's education, and comes down severely on the ornamental kind of boarding-school education that does not train the mind. This was also Oliver Goldsmith's method of social criticism in *Citizen of the World*. Lawrence's novel takes up reports of the matrilinear system of property inheritance among the Nairs of Kerala and imagines a society without marriage. Where property is not inherited through the male line, female chastity loses its importance and a double standard of morality can be dispensed with. The novel is thus a critique of a patriarchal society where chastity is posited as a virtue precisely on the ground of property inheritance. 'Consider', Dr Johnson had said to Boswell, 'of what importance to society the chastity of women is. Upon that all the property in the world depends. We hang a thief for stealing a sheep; but the unchastity of a woman transfers sheep and farm and all, from the right owner.'[10]

This satirical use of the travel tale or a foreigner's perspective was very different from the romantic evocation of the Orient in poetry – for example, in Coleridge's 'Kubla Khan', Shelley's *Prometheus Unbound*, Thomas Moore's *Lalla Rookh* and Southey's *The Curse of Kehama*. A great deal of this imaginative interest in India and the East generally can be traced to William Jones, whose work was diffused most widely in the 1790s through his *Asiatic Researches*. *The Missionary, an Indian Tale* (3 vols; 2nd edn. 1811), by Sydney Owenson, Lady Morgan, is a fictional distillation of Jones's influences, describing a Kashmiri princess and a Christian missionary. Warren Hastings, Jane Austen's family friend and an early admirer of *Pride and Prejudice*, shared in this new enthusiasm for Indian myth and literature. He introduced a newly translated *Bhagavad Gita* by saying that long after the British domination of India has ended the Hindu scriptures would continue to be read.

But Jane Austen's novels reflect neither the scholarly nor the orientalist interest in the East. If her characters establish a relationship with the expanding world outside it is mainly through its contemporary relevance to Britain. Sir Thomas Bertram's life-style in *Mansfield Park* is evidently dependent on his overseas investments, and at some point he 'found it expedient to go to Antigua himself for the better arrangement of his affairs' (ch. 3). His sudden return from the West Indies after nearly a year was considered an unmitigated disaster for the young people at home, who had been free from all parental constraints in the meantime. The prospect of long dull evenings at home and no hope of staging *Lover's Vows*, the play they had been rehearsing with much emotional involvement, depressed them considerably. Only Fanny Price could tell Edmund with honesty, 'The evenings do not appear long to me. I love to hear my uncle talk of the West Indies. I could listen to him for an hour together. It entertains me more than many other things have done – but then I am unlike other people I dare say' (ch. 21).

In England, both in life and in literature, the ex-colonial's talk of his experiences overseas has traditionally been considered boring (Thackeray's Joseph Sedley epitomises the phenomenon) but Jane Austen unashamedly gives two of her heroines quite different attitudes. Fanny Price is as much unlike the smart Crawfords as Elinor Dashwood is unlike Marianne and Willoughby. Instead of being cynical or making about other people's experiences in the tropics, Fanny and Elinor are eager to know the details. Fanny is apologetic about her naïve curiosity. Having ventured one evening to ask her uncle about the slave trade, she is so embarrassed by the 'dead silence that followed' that she never broaches the topic again:

> And while my cousins were sitting by without speaking a word, or seeming at all interested in the subject, I did not like – I thought it would appear as if I wanted to set myself off at their expense, by shewing a curiosity and pleasure in his information which he must wish his own daughters to feel.   (*Mansfield Park*, ch. 21)

Fanny's interest in slavery is nothing unusual because the slave trade was a much-discussed subject in Jane Austen's time. Raised in Parliament by Wilberforce in 1788 (when Jane Austen was thirteen) the subject continued to be hotly debated for twenty years before a bill providing for the abolition of the slave trade in the British colonies received the royal assent in 1807. Fanny's question articulated after the Abolition Bill had been passed indicates that the act of Parliament did not change everything overnight. That the slave-trade controversy was very much a topic of ordinary conversation can be seen in *Emma* too, in the reaction of Mrs Elton to Jane Fairfax when she talks of her future career as the sale 'not quite of human flesh but human intellect'! Literal-minded Mrs Elton, never at a loss for words, promptly replies, 'Oh my dear; human flesh! You quite shock me; if you mean a fling at the slave trade, I assure you Mr Suckling was always rather a friend to the abolition' (ch. 35). Jane's response which equates the governess trade with the slave trade, is a telling comment on the working-conditions prevalent in this profession and the socially generated self-pity of the women compelled to take it up: 'I did not mean, I was not thinking of the slave-trade ... governess-trade, I assure you, was all that I had in view; widely different, certainly as to the guilt of those who carry it on; but as to the greater misery of the victims, I do not know where it lies'.

In *Mansfield Park* the Crawfords and the Bertram girls live in a sealed and static space, totally self-obsessed and completely unheeding of the world outside, where a war was going on and where slaves worked on plantations to ensure the comfort and elegance of their lives in a country mansion. Jane Austen quietly draws a distinction between the limited world that Sir Bertram's daughters and sons inhabit and the quality of Fanny's mind, which can open out to issues beyond the self.

If Fanny Price in *Mansfield Park* is lonely in her heightened consciousness, so is Anne Elliot in *Persuasion*. While for Anne the sea stands for the expanding world of new experience and adventure, her baronet father is caught up in the self-reflexive world of mirrors and his anxiety to retain the class privileges that economic reality can no longer sustain. Sir Walter inhabits the past, refusing to face the fact that the balance of power is shifting from those whose rights are based on inheritance to those who are making Britain's fortunes at sea and in the colonies. In this novel, the year of the action, 1814, is very close to the year of composition – 1816. *Persuasion*, incidentally, is the only novel of Jane Austen that has such an explicit historical context. While Sir Walter defensively shields himself from history, concentrating on his complexion, which can only be saved from the effects of age by insulation from sunlight and open space, his daughter has been keeping up with Britain's maritime achievements. When Admiral Croft is mentioned as a possible tenant for the Elliot family seat, which Sir Walter can no longer maintain, his quiet and unobtrusive daughter seems to have all the information about this war hero: 'He is the rear admiral of the white. He was in the Trafalgar action, and has been in the East Indies since' (ch. 3). Sir Walter is completely indifferent to these facts, and merely speculates on the admiral's appearance: 'Then I take it for granted ... that his face is about as orange as the cuffs and capes of my livery.' The comic exaggeration of Sir Walter's traits is a device to freeze in a grotesque unreality of the class that refused to face the changing demands of history and geography.

Although Anne Elliot's fate relegates her to a passive role amidst the smug and static men who cannot see beyond their own immediate context and young ladies living merely to be 'fashionable, happy and merry', she hankers for the wider world of action where men and women have mobility across the globe. Mrs Croft's account of her travels, in the course of which she has 'crossed the Atlantic four times and ... been once to the East Indies and back again; and only once, besides being in different places about home: Cork, and Lisbon and Gibraltar' (ch. 8), fascinates her. Moreover Mrs Croft stands out in the crowd of bourgeois ladies in her assertion of physical sturdiness, defying the expected feminine qualities of frailty and dependence: 'Thank God! I have been blessed with an excellent health and no climate disagrees with me.' She embodies a code of behaviour that challenges the much-hallowed ideals of the chivalric male and the delicate lady. When her brother expresses his scruples about carrying women on board his ship because of their inconvenience, she admonishes him, 'I hate to hear you talking so, like a fine gentleman, and as if women were all fine ladies instead of rational creatures.'

This echoes Elizabeth Bennet's insistence that she is not an 'elegant female' but a 'rational creature' (*Pride and Prejudice*, ch. 19). In her physical vitality Elizabeth too defies the code that values debility and frailty. One also recalls Jane Austen's indulgent description of young Catherine Morland, who played cricket, rolled down slopes, and hated confinement and cleanliness. Jane Austen seems to have an unarticulated image of a fully individualised woman who is physically and mentally unrestricted, more mobile, more aware, more herself that the fainting creature in need of male protection and totally without a mind, an image that the conduct books and popular fiction had combined to idealise. Mrs Croft's regret – 'I never went beyond the Streights – and never was in the West Indies. We do not call Bermuda or Bahama, you know, the West Indies' – is met by Mrs Musgrove with silence (*Persuasion*, ch. 8). Having never spared a thought for anything beyond her family and the immediate neighbourhood, she 'had not a word to say is dissent; she could not accuse herself of having ever called them anything in the whole course of her life'.

Even those who had never been to the West Indies could have financial interest there – a fact underlined in the sub-plot of *Persuasion*. Mrs Smith's husband had bought a small estate in the West Indies, which since his death had been 'under a sort of sequestration of the payment of its own incumbrances' (ch. 21), and which the chivalrous Captain Wentworth restores to her by 'writing for her, acting for her and seeing her through all the petty difficulties of the case' (ch. 24). So by the end of the novel Mrs Smith has an 'improvement of income' through an investment made in a distant colony.

Jane Austen never uses foreign settings in her novels; her quality of ironic mimesis needed the restrictive frame of the England that she knew. We know that she warned her niece Anna, who had literary ambitions, against the danger of following her fictional characters to an unknown territory: 'You had better not leave England. Let the Portmans go to Ireland, but as you know nothing of the manners there, you had better not go with them.'[11] Jane Austen does not even have recourse to the familiar fictional device of shipping the inconvenient characters off to the colonies. Defoe has sent Moll Flanders to Virginia for repentance and rehabilitation, and Richardson in *Pamela* had banished the unfortunate Sally Godfrey to Jamaica to save Mr B. from further temptations. (Incidentally, a reformed Sally subsequently 'Sent a little negro boy, about ten years old' to wait upon her illegitimate daughter, who was being educated by Mr B. in England.) By the nineteenth century this had become a very common plot device, and dozens of examples can be cited from Victorian fiction (for example, *Adam Bede*, *Hard Times*, *David Copperfield*), where the existence of the colonies greatly facilitates the fictional closure. In Jane Austen only two characters are found fit for such an exile, but the country remains unspecified. In *Mansfield Park*, Maria Bertram and Mrs Norris have to remove themselves to 'an establishment being formed for them in another country, remote and private, where shut up together with little society, on one side no affection, on the other no judgment, it may be reasonably supposed their tempers became their mutual punishment' (ch. 48). The colonies also furnished the nineteenth-century English novel with the figure of the heiress from the West

Indies (Bertha Mason in *Jane Eyre*, the mulatto heiress
in *Vanity Fair*), but Jane Austen makes no use of such
a character, possibly because such geographical mobility
was still quite rare for women.

In *Northanger Abbey* Jane Austen mocks her heroine
for investing the countries outside England with romance
and exaggerated charm on the one hand and sinister horror
of untold vices on the other – an impression obviously
based on her reading of gothic novels. Henry Tilney, who
is the ironic intelligence of the novel and ought to be less
insular than the inexperienced Catherine, also in a way
corroborates Catherine's view by claiming reason, order
and normalcy for England alone: 'Remember that we are
English, that we are Christians', he solemnly proclaims,
in order to prove to Catherine that English society lacks
the darkness and mystery that might exist abroad. Tilney's
argument may not be entirely free of playfulness. Nevertheless, whether the author's voice is to be identified with
Tilney's or not, the fact remains that Jane Austen's fictional world is firmly located in the south of England. Just
as 'Catherine dared not doubt beyond her own country,
and even of that, if hard pressed, would have yielded the
northern and western extremities' (ch. 25), Jane Austen
dared not expand her actual fictional space beyond a dozen
counties in the southern England of which she had first-
hand experience, even though her knowledge and interest
extended to areas far outside this empirical boundary.

Her last completed novel, *Persuasion*, where the sea
is a major presence, seems to be on the verge of widening
out beyond the shores of the British Isles. Anne Eliot does
not have a fixed home at the end of the novel, but 'she
gloried in being a sailor's wife'. Diametrically opposed to
Persuasion in terms of space is its immediate predecessor.
Not only is *Emma* a totally landlocked novel (the heroine
confesses to never having seen the sea) but the entire action
except the Box Hill picnic takes place within an area of

two square miles. In every other novel of Jane Austen there are several shifts of locale. In *Northanger Abbey* the plot requires the heroine to move away from her home in Fullerton (Wiltshire) to Bath, then to Northanger Abbey, and finally to return home for the resolution. *Sense and Sensibility* features at least four shifts, each involving a long journey: from Norland Park in Sussex to Barton Park in Devon, the to London, and subsequently to Cleveland in Somerset. In *Pride and Prejudice* only the first of the three volumes is located entirely in Longbourn (Hertfordshire). The second volume is full of movement: first Jane goes to London to stay with the Gardiners, then Elizabeth accepts the invitation to visit Charlotte Collins at Hunsford in Kent. After an eventful six weeks there, Elizabeth returns through London, from where Jane accompanies her home. Barely four weeks after this Elizabeth leaves home again to travel northward with the Gardiners to Derbyshire – a journey that includes the momentous visit to Pemberley. The last volume is full of bustle, with the location shifting between London and Longbourn. Finally, Elizabeth's marriage involves an uprooting from Hertfordshire to distant Derbyshire.

In fact, almost all Jane Austen's heroines have to move to another district when they marry. The only exception is *Emma* who does not even have to move from her house to Knightley's estate in the neighbourhood because he comes to live with her. *Mansfield Park* is also to some extent a spatially static novel, because the house of the title symbolises the order and grace of which the heroine is the true inheritor. But to understand its value she has to move away from it once – to the squalor and disorder of Portsmouth. The incessant noise and lack of ceremony in her parents' house make her long for 'the elegance, propriety, regularity, harmony – and perhaps, above all, the peace and tranquillity of Mansfield' (ch. 39). Whatever the opinion of the modern reader about this difference (the

Portsmouth interlude obviously invites accusations of
snobbery and elitism today), it is evident that certainly
for Fanny, and less certainly for Jane Austen, the focus
is more on the moral and aesthetic quality of life than
on the material and economic factors that create or deny
elegance. Fanny's three month separation from the Bertram estate and the journeys at the beginning and end
of it are an important element in the narrative structure
of *Mansfield Park*.

Unlike the five novels in which shifts of location and
plot dynamics are interconnected, *Emma* is situated entirely in Highbury; London, which is sixteen miles away,
is made to appear rather distant. The sense of being closed
in is emphasised by Mr Woodhouse's anxiety about
draughts through open doors and the danger that is thought
to threaten women walking unescorted beyond the shrubberies. Donwell Abbey is only twenty minutes' brisk walk
away even for a delicate creature such as Jane Fairfax,
but Emma insists, 'it is too far indeed to be walking quite
alone. Let my father's servant go with you. Let me order
the carriage' (ch. 42). Once, while venturing to walk alone,
Harriet is accosted by gypsies and, even though they may
not have meant any harm, a situation is created in which
she needs a male to rescue her. Randalls, the residence
of the Westons, is only about a mile away from Emma's
home, Hartfield, and Donwell Abbey – Mr Knightley's
estate – perhaps twice this distance, but we are told that
Emma and her father have not visited Mr Knightley for
two years. Box Hill, barely six miles away, is a picnic spot
that Emma has never seen before the disastrous outing
there. To be settled and satisfied seems to be the ideal,
because Frank Churchill's remark 'I am sick of England,
and would leave to-morrow if I could' is considered by
Emma to be the tantrum of a spoilt young man who has
had too much 'prosperity and indulgence' (ch. 42). The
war between Britain and France over two decades may

have resulted in an emphasis on values that were seen as distinctly British, an emphasis that Mr Knightley shares with Emma in his condemnation of Frank Churchill's ways as more French than British. Unlike *Persuasion*, where the vitality of society is seen to have shifted, as it were, from the land to the sea, *Emma* is almost a paean to the perfection of culture achieved by the traditional English landlord untroubled and uncontaminated by anything outside the idyllic rural setting of his own home. Emma feels a 'honest pride and complacency' as she walks the grounds of Donwell Abbey:

> its ample gardens stretching down to meadows washed by a stream ... and its abundance of timber in rows and avenues, which neither fashion, nor extravagance has rooted up ... [the house] was just what it ought to be ... and Emma felt an increasing respect for it, as the residence of a family of such true gentility, untainted in blood and understanding.   (ch. 42)

Although part of the pleasure of reading *Emma* lies in sensing the carefully concealed gaps of irony that separate the author's from her heroine's perception, the rapture of the heroine at this point is often unequivocally attributed to the author as well: 'It was a sweet view – sweet to the eye and the mind, English verdure, English culture, English comforts, seen under a sun bright without being oppressive.' If Emma's sense of exultation is an unconscious projection of her desire to own this view one day, it seems to be mediated through the author's appreciation of this acme of English agrarian culture nurtured and refined through taste and hard work.

The hard work, however, is not very visible in *Emma*, although we know that Mr Knightley is a conscientious landlord whose closeness to his bailiff, William Larkin, is something of a joke in his social circle. His friendship with his tenant farmer Robert Martin also shows an appreciation of the value of honest labour that Emma in her idleness would never understand. Still, it is possible to see why radical critics such as David Aers and Roger Sales see *Emma* as celebrating the world of the rich landowning gentry to the total exclusion of the majority of the population:

> She waves a magic wand and the mass of the population vanishes into thin air, leaving only the fruits of their labour for the likes of Mr Knightley to appropriate. You can walk around 'large and populous Highbury' or walk around Mr Knightley's estate and never see a labourer. The system of production is so natural that we are persuaded that it needs no workers.[12]

Despite traces of authorial irony, *Emma* strikes one as a predominantly conservative text in which the existing order and social boundaries are seen as natural and good. Harriet and Robert Martin's marriage is a convenient reconfirmation of class identity, and the two outsiders, Jane Fairfax and Frank Churchill, are coupled and eliminated from the enclosed and static world of Highbury so that normalcy can return. At the end of the book one can visualise the continuity of social life in Highbury, now led by Emma Knightley, whose elevation through the ownership of two estates might inspire awe even in an upstart such as Mrs Elton. The motif of spatial enclosure, repeated so often in the novel, becomes in a way a metaphor for stasis of other kinds as well, temporarily threatened by Frank Churchill but ultimately prevailing at the end. It may be recalled that both Mr Woodhouse and Emma feel uneasy about 'this young man' Frank Churchill who opens too many doors and whose disregard of class almost borders on 'an inelegance of mind'. But is the observation of either the father or the daughter a reliable indicator of the author's views? The fact that reality is filtered through Emma's consciousness means the author's voice cannot readily be disentangled from that of her heroine. Particularly on the question of class we are involved in intractable paradoxes.

The question of class never comes to the surface so sharply in Jane Austen's other novels as it does in *Emma*. Her novels always focus on the upper middle class and the gentry, and, even when her characters live in strained circumstances, as Mrs Dashwood does with her three daughters – or, worse, as the Prices of Portsmouth do – they never present the author with quite the kind of social problem that Robert Martin poses for Emma:

> The yeomanry are precisely the order of people with whom I can have nothing to do. A degree or two lower . . . I might hope to be useful to their families in some way or other. But a farmer is . . . in one sense as much above my notice as in every other he is below.
>
> (ch. 4)

In fact, except in *Emma*, and to some extent in *Mansfield Park*, there is hardly any ambiguity about Jane Austen's position on class. While it would be absurd to expect her totally to disregard the hierarchical structure of the society of her time, nevertheless in every confrontation between the aristocracy the middle class she unerringly aligns herself with the latter. In *Pride and Prejudice* the middle-class Bennets and Gardiners compel the upper-class Darcys and de Bourghs to take them seriously. Elizabeth suffers from no sense of inferiority on her first visit to Rosings because 'mere stateliness of money and rank she thought she could witness without trepidation', only 'extraordinary talents or miraculous virtue' might inspire awe (ch. 29). Later, when Lady Catherine gives class difference as a reason why Elizabeth cannot marry Darcy, Elizabeth's spirited reply is 'He is a gentleman, I am a gentleman's daughter,

so far we are equal.' The definition of a gentleman is the
same here as in *Persuasion*, where Sir Walter Elliot insists
that only those who live on unearned income from inherited land without taking up a profession deserve this appel-
lation. Reminded of a gentleman called Mr Wentworth
who had once lived in the neighbourhood, he responds,
'Wentworth? Oh ay! Mr Wentworth, the curate of Monk-
ford. You misled me by the term *gentleman*. I thought
you were speaking of some man of property' (ch. 3). When
Lady Catherine in *Pride and Prejudice* hints at the low
social connections of Elizabeth's mother (one brother an
attorney and the other in trade), her strictures are under-
mined by the fact that the Gardiners – the brother in trade
and his wife – are two of the most positive characters in
the novel and receive the novelist's full support as indicated
in the concluding lines. In *Northanger Abbey* the Mor-
lands, with their common-sense views, triumph over the
Tilneys, who own an abbey. In *Sense and Sensibility* the
impoverished Dashwoods counter the obstinacy of the
moneyed and proud Mrs Ferrar. In *Persuasion* the rising
professional class is obviously privileged over the decadent
aristocracy. All the titled people, from Sir Walter to 'the
Dowager Viscountess Dalrymple and her daughter, the
Honourable Miss Carteret' are drawn with comic exaggeration. Anne's indifference to 'rank and connection' is
clearly the normative position in this novel.

In Jane Austen's letters we find sharp and adverse comments on *Fitzalbini*, a rather reactionary novel by her contemporary and acquaintance Samuel Egerton Brydges,
who passionately lamented the 'deterioration of the higher
classes of landed gentry'[13] owing to Pitt's encouragement
of mercantile enterprise. Brydges believed that men who
had made money in trade were 'a miserable lot' – a view
reminiscent of that of Sir Walter in *Persuasion*, whom Jane
Austen caricatures. Generally Jane Austen sees the complex process of change far too clearly to side with those

who insisted rigidly to maintain the old class divisions. Raymond Williams characterises the society of Jane Austen's novels as 'an acquisitive high bourgeois society at the point of its most evident interlocking with agrarian capitalism that is itself mediated by inherited titles and the making of family names'.[14] At the same time the country's economy was expanding through overseas trade and development of the colonies, and in most of Jane Austen's novels – traditionally seen as depicting a stable, static and limited world – the pulls and pressures that enhanced social mobility are not only visible but are woven into the plot with the novelist's implicit endorsement. In *Persuasion* the dice are obviously loaded in favour of those who have risen through individual effort. Eight years before the beginning of the novel Wentworth was 'a young man who had nothing but himself to recommend him, and no hopes of attaining affluence but in the chances of a most uncertain profession, and no connexion to secure even his farther rise in that profession' (ch. 4). By the end of the novel 'Captain Wentworth with five and twenty thousand pounds and as high in his profession as merit and activity would place him' is equal to anyone in England and can marry 'the daughter of a foolish spendthrift baronet' with Jane Austen's blessing (ch. 24).

But in *Emma* the preservation of class hierarchy becomes an important issue, and marriages instead of being means of social and spatial mobility become devices for rigid reconfirmation of class and space enclosures. Harriet's marriage with Mr Knightley's tenant farmer means that 'the intimacy between her and Emma must sink'. However much Mr Knightley might value Robert Martin at work, he recognises that socially they must not interact – 'His rank in society I would alter if I could which is saying a great deal, I assure you, Emma' (ch. 54) – because social boundaries are seen as inviolable, almost divinely ordained. The issue of authorial irony becomes most

thorny in the last few pages of the novel, where, according
to many interpretations, Emma's moral education reaches
its completion. The long-awaited resolution of the mystery
surrounding Harriet's birth is resolved when 'she is proved
to be the illegitimate daughter of a rich tradesman', sham-
ing Emma's attempts to connect her with the 'gentlemen'
in her social circle: 'The stain of illegitimacy unbleached
by nobility or wealth, would have been a stain indeed'
(ch. 55). The words 'blood', 'stain' and 'taint' are used
more than once in the novel, emphasising the concern that
was felt for preserving the purity of the blood of the English
gentry. Earlier, when Emma is in raptures over Donwell
Abbey, she reflects on the 'untainted blood' of the Knight-
leys as one of their supreme achievements, and at the end
she is thankful that she has failed in her efforts to find
a gentleman husband for a mere tradesman's daughter:
'Such was the blood of gentility which Emma had been
so ready to vouch for' (ch. 55). The recurring language
of purity and pollution testifies to Emma's anxiety to pre-
serve social boundaries. The middle class could move
upwards through marriage, but the code within which Jane
Austen operated did not permit descent below a certain
social and economic level. The narrative of *Emma* closes
in upon itself, offering a contrast to her next novel, *Persuasion*, where the movement is outward. The two great
houses, Hartfield and Donwell Abbey, merge at the end
of *Emma*, merely repeating a union between the two families that has occurred once already. Consequently there
is no expansion of the family or social circle. In *Persuasion*,
on the other hand, the heroine marries outside her social
class; she not only glories in being a sailor's wife' but also
happily becomes part of gradually expanding fraternity of
sea-faring people who do without the stability of a fixed
home. Considering the importance of houses in Jane Austen's earlier novels (two of which take their titles from
them), the relinquishment of a fixed home in *Persuasion*

seems a major departure.

Jane Austen's novels involve us in insoluble problems about the breadth/narrowness of her vision, the humanistic/hierarchical basis of her values, and the degree of mobility/stasis in her narrative design. On all these issues, the evidence on one side of the argument can almost always be countered by the evidence on the other side. *Emma* is the greatest stumbling-block to the theory that Jane Austen's novels show her views on social and moral questions gradually developing into those of *Persuasion*, where they are least class-bound. The indeterminacy is manipulated through ironic focusing, the irony being not always against others but sometimes turned inward.

4 'Crowd in a little room'

Oh! Miss Woodhouse, the comfort of being sometimes alone!

Emma

Could they be perpetrated, without being known, in a country like this, where social and literary intercourse is in such footing where every man is surrounded by a neighbourhood of voluntary spies . . . .

Northanger Abbey

Fanny Price, who was 'disposed to think the influence of London very much at war with all respectable attachments' (*Mansfield Park*, ch. 45), may have been partly voicing the author's view on the subject. Although London and Bath often feature in Jane Austen's novels as settings for developments in the plot – serving to bring people together, to separate or to regroup them, or to dislocate them from the familiar context – the important events and the final resolutions of the novels always take place in the countryside, which provides the stable, unhurried norm of her fictional world. Her characters are occasionally made to visit the urban centres because displacement from their home surroundings can set the plot in motion, making room for complexities in human interaction; but none of her major characters derives his or her durable values from the cities. Only the Crawfords have been brought up in London, and this is responsible not only for their glamour and wit but also their underlying brittleness and falsity, which proves such a disruptive influence in the life of Mansfield. To view the town and the country as morally opposing entitites has indeed been an age-old literary convention, but in Jane Austen's case the practice obtains further validation through her own emotional attachment to the countryside. We know that, like Anne Elliot, the heroine of her last novel, Jane Austen 'persisted in a very determined, though very silent disinclination for Bath' (*Persuasion*, ch. 14). She was miserable when, after spending the first twenty-six years of her life in the quiet rectory of Steventon in Hampshire, she had to move to Bath because of a sudden decision made by her parents. Two of her heroines also make the journey to Bath. Catherine Morland, very young and eager for experience, finds Bath exciting. But Anne Elliot – an older heroine, created in Jane Austen's maturity – feels out of place in the social rituals of a fashionable resort and can only sigh that her father 'should feel no degradation' in changing his residence from the spacious country seat Kellynch Hall to a cramped place whose walls are 'perhaps thirty feet asunder'. Edmund Bertram's scepticism about the 'proportion of virtue to vice' in London is expressed categorically in *Mansfield Park*: 'We do not look in great cities for our best morality' (ch. 9). In *Sense and Sensibility* the Dashwood sisters, particularly Marianne, long for 'the air, the liberty and quiet of the country' after being in London for more than two months.

The three qualities that Elinor and Marianne miss in London – openness, peace and freedom – although traditionally associated with the country, and present in its physical landscape, are actually not very evident in the mental climate of the close-knit communities we find in Jane Austen's novels. The social interaction is so intimate that it borders on the oppressive. It is not certain that

Jane Austen is always creating this oppressive effect deliberately, because there are passages where the thrust is
in the opposite direction – where the small, caring and
closed world is imbued with positive qualities. The England
she really knew and valued was largely agrarian, governed
in a paternalistic fashion by the land-owning gentry and
aristocracy. In her novels she seldom ventures beyond the
pastoral south of England to the industrialising north. If
her advice to her niece Anna against taking her fictional
characters out of England is any indication, Jane Austen
believed that a writer ought to stay within the territory
she fully knew. The territory Jane Austen knew consisted
of self-sufficient rural units with their own church, shops
and apothecary, and presiding over these communities,
a few land-owning families with large and comfortable
family seats, symbolic of traditional English society. In
at least three of her novels these great houses form the
hub of activity – Hartfield and Donwell Abbey in *Emma*,
Kellynch and Uppercross in *Persuasion*, and the house that
gives its name to *Mansfield Park*. In *Northanger Abbey*
and *Pride and Prejudice* the great mansions Northanger
Abbey and Pemberley are not at the centre of the narrative
but the heroines find their way to them by the end of the
narrative. *Sense and Sensibility* begins when the Dashwood
sisters are dispossessed of their father's estate of Norland.
But by the end at least one of the heroines is compensated
by the acqustion – through marriage – of another estate
and mansion at Delaford, so impressive that even the present owner of Norland estate is awed by it. 'His property
here, his place, his house, everything in such respectable
and exellent condition! – and his woods! – I have not seen
such timber anywhere in Dorsetshire', exclaims John
Dashwood, an expert in the evaluation of material costs
(ch. 50). In Jane Austen's world the parsonages and houses
belonging to the smaller gentry are also comfortable, with
wide lawns, gardens and shrubberies. When Mrs Dash-

wood in her reduced circumstances moves to a small cottage, we are told that even that has two parlours of sixteen feet square, and, if her family felt cramped inside, there were fields and woods outside in which they could take long walks.

On one level Jane Austen's novels, with all their leisured lives, large houses, open prospects, rolling lawns, gardens and trees, give us a sense of space. Yet on another level it is possible to feel closed in, oppressed by a lack of privacy in this close-knit society. This feeling does not come from the presence of domestic labour, although it would have been quite natural at a time when servants were plentiful. Curiously enough, servants are scarcely visible in Jane Austen's novels. Mrs Bennet takes offence at Mr Collins' polite inquiry about her daughters' culinary skills, because she can afford servants to do the cooking. Even the impoverished Mrs Dashwood can afford two servants inside the house other than the ones that must have seen to the garden or the carriage. At a time when there was no electricity and no piped water, the elegant life-style of the gentry had obviously to be supported by a numerous work-force. But in Jane Austen's novels we never get a strong sense of their presence. Only a few of the service people are named – Mrs Whitaker, the housekeeper at Sotherton (*Mansfield Park*); James, Mr Woodhouse's coachman (*Emma*) – and even these are never concretised as human beings.

If we feel oppressed, the reasons are less tangible. It is characteristic of Jane Austen that in surroundings that offer plenty of physical space, she portrays a society that closely restricts mental space – particularly of the women, who are allowed very little solitude or freedom. Many of the crucial events take place indoors, often in the presence of a large number of people. Frequently the plot moves forward through overheard conversation; rumour plays a large part in transmitting news, and gossip is the staple

of life. The sense of being hedged in, being watched and
discussed by the whole community, characterises most of
her novels. Paradoxically, it also forces her characters –
at least the central ones – to be very private. What are
the areas of life where thoughts, feelings and information
can be shared, and what are the areas where secrecy is
desirable, forms one of the implied moral debates of her
work. This tension between the public and the private areas
of life, in their many subtle variations, provides a narrative
balance in all her six novels. The survival and development
of the private individual in a very close-knit society that
affords little solitude seems to be one of the underlying
concerns of Jane Austen's fiction.

   In such a society letters are not private documents either
when they are being written or when they are being
received. This is how a normal evening at Netherfield is
described: 'Mr Darcy was writing, and Miss Bingley, seated
near him, was watching the progress of the letter' (*Pride
and Prejudice* (ch. 10). Most letters when received are read
out in the family or the communication is shared with
friends. In the same novel, when a note comes to Jane
from Netherfield, Mrs Bennet is impatient to know about
its contents: 'Well, Jane, who is it from? What is it about?
What does it say? Well, Jane, make haste and tell us; make
haste my love' (ch. 7). In *Emma* Mr Weston takes the
liberty of opening his wife's letter and reading it before
she does. He cannot wait till the contents are shared with
everyone present: '"Read it, read it," said he, "it will
give you pleasure; only a few lines – will not take you
long; read it to Emma." The two ladies looked over it
together' (ch. 35). Like Frank Churchill's letters, the letters from Jane Fairfax are also the common property of
Highbury, and these are shared by Miss Bates so gener-
ously with all her visitors that Emma dares to visit her
only after calculating that the time is 'just now quite safe
from any letter from Jane Fairfax' (ch. 19). Frank Chur-

chill's final explanatory letter to Mrs Weston (ch. 50) is not only read by Emma, but she has to subject it to a post-mortem by going over it a second time with Mr Knightley; his critical comments reflect darkly on the writer, who never meant it to be seen by either of them. While this sharing of letters may be justified as evidence of the cohesiveness of an organic society, its bond of fellow-feeling and concern, by a sleight of vision it appears as a rude invasion of privacy, as unforgivable encroachment upon private relationships. Jane Austen's laconic mode makes it possible to invest these acts with an aura of non-committal detachment. Highbury keeps a watch on Jane Fairfax's habits of correspondence presumably because people are interested in her welfare. In *Persuasion* Anne's reading of a letter from William Elliot to a third party, Mr Smith, although admittedly 'a violation of the laws of honour', is an important step towards the resolution of the plot, and seems to be condoned by the author. Anne Elliot reasons with herself 'that no one ought to be judged or to be known by such testimonies, that no private correspondence could bear the eye of others' (ch. 21), but she reads the letter nevertheless, and lets its contents influence her opinion of Mr Elliot.

Reading a letter meant for another person is a form of eavesdropping, an activity that is fairly common and appears generally to be deemed acceptable in the communities that Jane Austen depicts:

> Elizabeth passed quietly out of the room, Jane and Kitty followed, but Lydia stood her ground, determined to hear all she would; and Charlotte, detained first by the civility of Mr Collins ... and then by a little curiosity, satisfied herself with walking to the window, and pretending not to hear. (*Pride and Prejudice*, ch. 20)

No, no, they were shut up in the drawing room together,

and all I heard was only by listening at the door.   (*Sense and Sensibility*, ch. 38)

I do not ask you what the Colonel has been saying to you, for though upon my honour, I *tried* to keep out of hearing, I could not help catching enough to understand his business.   (Ibid., ch. 40)

Apart from such deliberate eavesdropping out of curiosity, there are several instances of inadvertent overhearing, crucial acts upon which the plots of these novels hinge. Elizabeth's overhearing of Darcy's judgement on her ('She is tolerable; but not handsome enough to tempt me') is the starting-point of her tense relationship with him, which provides the forward movement of the plot in *Pride and Prejudice*. If Wentworth had not dropped his pen when striving to overhear the gender debate between Anne Elliot and Captain Harville, the happy ending of *Persuasion* might not have been possible.

The crowded rooms and close proximity that make such overhearing possible also provide a kind of solitude and privacy. Catherine Morland and Henry Tilney forge an intimacy through the playful subversion of routine ballroom talk in a room full of noise and people. When Elinor Dashwood wants to have a private conversation with Lucy she chooses a crowded room: 'Miss Dashwood now judged, she might safely, under the shelter of . . . noise introduce the interesting subject without any risk of being heard at the card table' (*Sense and Sensibility*, ch. 23). Anne Elliot's most intense feelings of solitude occur when she is playing the piano in the crowded living-room of Uppercross. Elinor Dashwood too has the capacity for retaining her solitude and bearing her private sorrow while actively participating in crowded social events because 'she did not adopt the method . . . employed by Marianne on a similar occasion, to augment and fix her sorrow by seeking silence, solitude and idleness' (*Sense and Sensibility*, ch. 19). Marianne is the only one of Jane Austen's heroines who in her romantic individualism openly spurns most social norms. All the other protagonists, including the quiet and solitary Fanny Price and Anne Elliot, possess the ability to retain their individuality while negotiating the demands of an interfering and insistent community. Curiously, however, Marianne, who values privacy very highly, in a way forfeits it by being so unreserved. By 'concealing nothing' she makes herself vulnerable, while Elinor's caution seems justified in a world that is full of curious and insensitive people who constantly threaten to blur the distinction between the private and public spheres. Apart from the obvious examples such as Mrs Jennings, Miss Bates and Mrs Elton, there are numerous characters in Jane Austen's novels who in various ways violate the distinction – for example, Mr Collins, by introducing a pompous public idiom in the most intimate situations, and Wickham, by tricking Elizabeth into a fraudulent intimacy through private confessions made to a relative stranger. Darcy, by contrast, is a scrupulously private person who resents any invasion and refuses to play up to casual society. His comment to Elizabeth 'we neither of us perform to strangers' is really an acknowledgement of a quality he admires in Elizabeth.

Solitary reflection, something most of Jane Austen's heroines value, is a luxury that can be indulged only sparingly. Elizabeth Bennet on her return from Hunsford carries a burden of experience that has to be concealed from others, and longs for moments where she can be herself: 'Reflection must be reserved for solitary hours. Whenever she was alone, she gave way to it as the greatest relief' (*Pride and Prejudice*, ch. 37). Even Emma Woodhouse, who normally revels in being surrounded by people who admire her and whose lives she can manipulate, occasionally feels such a need. 'She wanted to be alone. Her mind was in a state of flutter and wonder which made it impossible

for her to be collected' (*Emma*, ch. 54). The most desperate cry comes from Jane Fairfax, the woman with no secure
place in life, constantly hedged in by prying and chattering
well-wishers: 'Oh! Miss Woodhouse, the comfort of being
sometimes alone' (ch. 41).

Fanny, the most sensitive of the heroines, leads a life
apart from the crowd, and her private space is concretised
in the rooms she inhabits – first the little white attic and
then the East Room, where 'she could go . . . after anything
unpleasant below, and find immediate consolation' (*Mansfield Park*). The symbolic use of a room as a woman's
private space is a recurrent device in nineteenth-century
fiction – in *Jane Eyre*, *Villette*, *Wuthering Heights*, *The
Mill on the Floss* and *Middlemarch*. Sometimes it is an
oppressive cloister, but more often (as frequently in Jane
Austen) it offers a pause in the narrative when the character may withdraw to collect herself and reflect on the doings
of others. When Elizabeth in *Pride and Prejudice* hears
the news that Lydia is after all to be married to Wickham,
she experiences mixed emotions: 'Elizabeth received her
congratulations among the rest, and then sick of the folly
took refuge in her own room that she might think with
freedom' (ch. 49). Earlier, after meeting Darcy and
Bingley at Pemberley, Elizabeth has reasons to be considerably agitated: 'Eager to be alone, and fearful of enquir-
ies or hints from her uncle and aunt . . . [she] hurried away
to dress' (ch. 44). Retiring to one's room becomes analogous to recovering one's wholeness, which is constantly
whittled away by the inquisitive glances and queries of
society. In *The Watsons* Emma Watson, who has no room
of her own, escapes to her father's sick-room from the
disturbing demands of the family: 'In *his* chamber, Emma
was at peace from the dreadful mortification of unequal
society and family discord – from the immediate endurance
of hard-hearted prosperity, low-minded conceit and
wrong-headed folly, engrafted on an outward disposition'

(last page of the unfinished novel). Even the socially confi-. dent Emma needs the sactuary of her bedroom to let down her guard: 'The hair was curled, and the maid sent away, and Emma sat down to think and be miserable' (*Emma*, ch. 16).

Later writers such as the Brontës and George Eliot who dealt with the passionate intensities of women outside the drawing-room carried the metaphorical use of the room further, sometimes to indicate a womb from which the character emerges to experience a rebirth of personality. Sometimes rooms, attics, corridors and passages symbolise the inner recesses of the mind where the dark secrets and the volatile emotions are concealed. The oblique use of architectural devices to enhance interiority is not so crucial in Jane Austen as it is in the later women writers. In Jane Austen's novels the houses generally seem to be well-lit and rationally laid out. The one exception is Northanger Abbey, where winding stairs and corridors lead to myster-ious rooms, and cabinets contain concealed drawers and cavities. By and large it is not the intricacy of a building but the secluded nature of a room that is emphasised in Jane Austen's work.

The room as the inviolate private space assumes such an importance because in Jane Austen's novels the world outside is relentlessly public. There is a foolproof network for the transmission of information and no individual is spared by it. It is not only the slightly comic or minor characters who indulge in gossip; even Captain Went-worth, the admirable hero of *Persuasion*, cannot contain his curiosity when he sees a new carriage arrive at the inn in Lyme. The waiter satisfies his curiosity by giving him all the details: 'a gentleman of large fortune – came in last night from Sidmouth, – dare say you heard the car-riage, Sir, while you were at dinner; and going on now for Crewkherne, on his way to Bath and London' (ch. 12). The curiosity of another character in the novel may be more justifiable because she is an invalid. Mrs Smith survives on a staple diet of gossip provided by her nurse and rationalises it as a way of getting to 'know one's species better': 'One likes to hear what is going on, to be *au fait* as to the newest modes of being trifling and silly. To me, who live so much alone, her conversation, I assure you is a treat' (ch. 17). In congratulating Anne on her impending marriage to Mr Elliot when Anne herself is completely unaware of any such possibility, she is acting as the conduit of Bath gossip. Mrs Smith admits to having heard the news from her friend Nurse Rooke, who heard it from Mrs Wallis, who must have heard it from Colonel Wallis, because she was confined to bed through childbirth and saw no one else. Anne, who is usually direct and uncurious in her dealings with people, asks with surprise, 'Colonel Wallis! you are acquainted with him?' (ch. 21). Mrs Smith answers complacently, 'No, It does not come to me in quite so direct a line as that: it takes a bend or two, but nothing of consequence. The stream is as good as at first; the little rubbish it collects in the turnings, is easily moved away'. Anne's admonition to her contains Jane Austen's comment on this entire texture of rumour and half-truth fabricated and sustained by an idle and closed society: 'Facts or opinions which are to pass through the hands of so many, to be misconceived by folly in one, and ignorance in another, can hardly have much truth left.'

Mrs Smith's curiosity may be overlooked as the perennial interest of the common folk in the private lives of the glamorous and the rich, an appetite that in our time is catered to by gossip columns, television and other branches of the mass media. But it is not only the underprivileged (there are very few of them in Jane Austen) who indulge in such prying. With the exception of a few sensitive individuals, the communities Jane Austen creates in her novels consist of people intensely involved in the lives of others who not only consider it their duty to be well-informed about their neighbours, but also to transmit all available information as soon as possible. Mrs Philips in *Pride and Prejudice* has only to talk to Mr Jones's shop boy on the street to find out that the doctor is not to send any more medicines to Netherfield, and she can correctly conclude that the Bennet sisters must be returning home that day. When Mrs Jennings in *Sense and Sensibility* wants to find out where Marianne and Willoughby have driven off to, 'she actually made her woman inquire of Mr Willoughby's groom' (ch. 13). Such instances of indirect fact-finding abound in Jane Austen's novels, whose closed-circuit world is neatly summarised by this passage from *Sanditon*:

> You must have heard me mention Miss Capper, the particular friend of my very particular friend Fenny Noyce; – now Miss Capper is extremely intimate with a Miss Darling, who is on terms of constant correspondene with Mrs Griffiths herself. Only a short chain between us and not a link wanting. (ch. 9)

Rumour is a very potent force in this claustrophobic world. One remembers how in *Pride and Prejudice* the report that Mr Bingley is to bring twelve ladies and seven gentlemen to the ball fires the imagination of the village – until he actually appears with two ladies and two gentlemen. In *Sense and Sensibility* Mrs Jennings feels cheated by the unexpected news regarding Lucy Steele and Edward Ferrars: 'There is no great wonder of their liking one another; but that matters should be brought so forward between them and nobody suspect it! *That* is strange' (ch. 57). It is the business of people to suspect, to anticipate, to comment and to advise. Jane's possible marriage to Bingley in *Pride and Prejudice* becomes a matter of general concern in Longbourn and even Charlotte Lucas begins to advise her how to play her cards to ensure a proposal.

When two persons get married or do not get married, the rest of the community feels compelled to applaud or dis- approve or take sides. Mrs Smith is a little annoyed with her friend Nurse Rooke 'for not being a very strenuous opposer of Sir Walter's making a second match' (*Persuasion*, ch. 21), when neither she nor Nurse Rooke has any direct contact with the gentleman in question. This presum- ably is the inevitable condition of an 'organic' community where each person's life is bound up with everyone else's.

That Jane Austen was not a consistent critic of this close- knit society with its chain of obligations, duties and shared values can be seen in many instances. Marianne Dash- wood's rejection of Mrs Jennings' sympathy – 'her good nature is not tenderness. All that she wants is gossip, and she only likes me now because I supply it' – is brushed aside by her more mature elder sister as an 'irritable refene- ment of her own mind' that makes her judge others too narrowly (*Sense and Sensibility*, ch. 31). What can be seen as interference becomes legitimised when regarded as part of a larger social system of interdependence and mutual support. The hierarchy inherent in the social organisation has to be accepted before its values can be fictionally cele- brated, and this is revealed in Jane Austen's attitudes to Pemberley and Donwell Abbey. Both Darcy and Knightley gain as human beings by managing and improving their estates well. Knightley undoubtedly gets bonus points for taking his duties 'as a magistrate' and 'as a farmer' seriously enough to spend whole evenings discussing them with his brother (*Emma*, ch. 12). Sir Walter Elliot is squarely cen- sured for dereliction of duties and Bingley mildly so for avoiding the responsibility of owning and managing an estate. It is important that by the end of *Pride and Prejudice* Bingley has shed his earlier indolence, which made those close to him wonder 'as he was now provided with a good house and the liberty of a manor ... whether he might not spend the remainder of his days at Netherfield, and leave the next generation to purchase' (ch. 41), and has actually gone on to purchase an 'estate in the neighbouring county to Derbyshire'. In the Jane Austen scale of values this is certainly an improvement, not only materially but also morally, because it indicates Bingley's willingness to take on responsibility and extend his patronage to others. In a society whose poise and stability are so dependent on the haromious functioning of the horizontal and vertical relationships between its members, it is inevitable that people's lives will impinge upon each other. 'Meddling' and 'concern', 'interference' and 'interest' can be interchangeable terms depending on the importance one attaches to the individual and his/her relationship with society. In Jane Austen's case the balance of emphasis does not remain constant but shifts subtly from novel to novel, always with a leavening of irony mediating the opposites.

Emma and *Persuasion* can be regarded as the two poles of her shifting position. All her novels deal with closed communities, but, as discussed in Chapter 3, *Emma* is her only novel set wholly within one small district. The action begins and ends in Highbury and even marriage cannot dislodge Emma from her permanent abode in Hartfield. The stasis is emphasised by inclement weather and closed doors at the beginning, and through the elimination of the two outsiders, Frank Churchill and Jane Fairfax, at the end. Hartfield, Randalls and Donwell Abbey, the three major scenes of action, are all within one or two miles of each other, but each movement seems to involve elaborate travel arrangements for the women. The roads outside the shrubbery seem unsafe for solitary walks. London is only sixteen miles away, but during the twelve months spanned by the novel only Frank Churchill, who is restless by nature, and Mr Knightley, who makes frequent trips on various unspecified errands, actually go there. Emma is the most fixed of Jane Austen's heroines: before the picnic on to Box Hill, which is only six miles away, she has never been there, and she has never seen the sea. Emma's father says, 'I have been for long perfectly convinced – that the sea is very rarely of use to anybody' (ch. 12).

This unchanging, landlocked ethos is conveyed not only through spatial references but also in terms of close and reiterative human interaction. One of Emma's problems is the smallness of her social circle, where one is doomed to meet the same people and go over the same topics of conversation for months together. Emma attempts to make life interesting by imagining situations, because there is very little scope for channelling her energy and wit. The problem that confronts most of Jane Austen's women, focused most sharply in the case of Emma Woodhouse, is that of leisure management. How can they fill up their time when according to the very definition of bourgeois femininity they cannot participate in the productive process and work structure of the society? Young women may spend their time acquiring the accomplishments prescribed by the conduct books and displaying them on social occasions, and look forward to marriage as giving them a purpose and place in life, but the lurking fear behind it all is expressed in Harriet Smith's horrified question when she learns that Emma does not want to marry: 'Dear me! but what shall you do? How shall you employ yourself when you grow old?' (ch. 10). Emma's complacent and perhaps self-deluded reply – 'If I know myself, Harriet, mine is an active, busy mind, with a great deal of independent resources. ... If I draw less, I shall read more; if I give up music, I shall take to carpet work' – really begs the question, because the items she lists are not work – they are merely pretexts for filling up vacant time. Married or unmarried, old or young, the problem of finding things to do remains the same. Only a young woman and her ways of spending time are of interest to the novelist and reader, because they lead to the climactic event of her life – marriage. John Knightley asks the crucial question about Emma – 'I wonder what will become of her' – which was echoed at the end of the nineteenth century (in *The Portrait of a Lady*) by Ralph Touchett's curiosity about what Isabel Archer would do with her life.

What can Emma do? She fills up the vacancy of her repetitive days and evenings with an active imagination, and much of the action is in her mind – and those of the other characters too. Emma imagines an affair between Jane Fairfax and Mr Dixon, and invests Jane with the aura of a romance heroine. Mrs Weston wishes a match between Emma and Frank Churchill, and, less ardently, one between Jane Fairfax and Mr Knightley. For a while Emma even imagines that she is in love with Frank Churchill. Among the three marriageable women and three marriageable men (four, if one includes Robert Martin), all possible combinations and relationships are either forged or imagined. In the almost absurd overgrowth of interconnections there are three different kinds of relationship: mutual attachment, one-way attachment and attachment that does not exist except in the imagination of others. It is to be noted that Harriet, the most labile of the group, is linked in some way or other with all four men: Mr Elton, Mr Knightley, Frank Churchill and Robert Martin. Jane Fairfax turns out to be the most well-defined personality, with the least number of attachments. In this hothouse atmosphere, unless a person is very determined and strong willed, the pressures of the group, constant interaction, gossip and rumour will predetermine the course of his or her life.

The tragedy of this stagnant world is echoed in Emma's lament after her first failure in match-making: 'Their being fixed, so absolutely fixed, in the same place was bad for each, for all three. Not one of them had the power of removal, or effecting any material change of society. They

must encounter each other and make the best of it' (ch.
17). At one point Mr Elton finds himself having to face
at dinner the woman he wanted to marry, the women who
would have liked to marry him, and the woman he had
actually married. Claustrophobia cannot go further. Yet
Emma, though herself a sufferer, cannot tolerate anyone
who chooses to stay out of this stifling circuit. When Jane
Fairfax refuses to indulge in gossip, 'Emma could not for-
give her' (chs 20 and 21), and Jane's lack of comment
on an absent person whom she has never seen elicits a
sharp rejoinder from Emma: 'you are silent, Miss Fairfax
– but I hope you mean to take an interest' (ch. 21). Emma's
centrality and power seem threatened by Jane's rejection
of the values of this network, which relies on the gathering,
transmission and dissection of news. 'News! Oh yes, I
always like news', admits Emma unabashedly.

The novel by Jane Austen that is furthest removed from
the landlocked static world of *Emma* is *Persuasion*, her
last novel, where the sea is the liberating element in the
narrative. This book contains more changes of location
than any of the earlier novels, and the motif of a house,
so important in the other novels both as a concrete object
and as a symbol of social stability, recedes into the background. Anne moves from Kellynch Hall to Uppercross
and then to the seaside resort of Lyme. Each of these
places embodies a different set of values and Anne goes
through the process of setting one against another eventually to sort out her own priorities. She also had to submit
to another lesson, of 'knowing our own nothingness
beyond our own circle' (ch. 6). After the rigid formality
and concern with surfaces at her father's house, the infor-
mality and confusion of Uppercross are a welcome change,
but the open friendliness of the naval officers in Lyme
Regis appeals to her most. Finally the inhabitants of all
three worlds converge in Bath, giving Anne an opportunity
to choose her orbit. Anne Elliot continues to have an

emotional attachment to her ancestral home, Kellynch
Hall, but at the end of the novel she marries a man without
a house, whose fortune lies at sea. This indicates a radical
shift in Jane Austen's position, because in her earlier writing a permanent abode is almost synonymous with a man's
moral and social worth. Even for someone as romantic
as Marianne, a man's attractiveness is much enhanced by
his possession of a substantial property (Willoughby shows
her over Allenham Court as his future home, and there
is the promise of another 'pretty little estate of his own'
in Somerset). A woman is allured by the details of physical
space in which to situate a man, and in her imagination
this is projected as a setting in which to see herself. Catherine Morland's avidness to see Tilney's vicarage and Fanny's
interest in Edmund's house – Thornton Tracy – are not
motivated by a desire for property, but are attempts to
visualise a man in the total context that will give him fixity
and solidity. To this extent houses are generally important
in Jane Austen's novels.

When Jane Austen wrote *Persuasion* the Navy had
recently brought glory to Britain through its victories in
the Napoleonic wars. The returning naval officers not only
were affluent but also introduced a new code of behaviour,
which valued loyalty and friendship above social rank and
money. Unlike in the earlier novels, where men and
women are seen as consumers and commodities respectively, in *Persuasion* there is a greater emphasis on equality
and partnership. It is this new sense of values that the
novel celebrates, and the sea becomes an effective metaphor for mobility, openness and emotional release. All
Jane Austen's other novels close *in* at the end, locating
the heroine in a particular spot and tying in all the loose
threads around this centre. *Persuasion* is the only novel
that opens *out*, moving away from enclosed space and
rootedness. Anne 'gloried in being a sailor's wife', we are
told at the end of *Persuasion*, and her happiness will not

be centred on a fixed hearth in England.

Although Jane Austen's last novel ends on a note of expansion rather than contraction, it is impossible to see this as the logical outcome of a steady progression in her novels. As has been pointed out by Tony Tanner, there is an essential dichotomy in Jane Austen's novels between stability and rootedness on the one hand and a restless energy on the other, and 'the tension and dialectic between them is ongoing'.[1] One of the reasons why her novels can be reread and have been reread over many generations is that this tension manifests itself in so many different patterns.

5 'Admiring Pope no more than is proper'

> ... for *one* morning I think you have done pretty
> well. You know what he thinks of Cowper and
> Scott; you are certain of his estimating their beau-
> ties as he ought, and you have received every
> assurance of his admiring Pope no more than is
> proper.
>
> *Sense and Sensibility*

In Umberto Eco's *The Name of the Rose* the detective
monk tells his young disciple Adso, 'Often books speak
of other books. Often a harmless book is like a seed that
will blossom into a dangerous book, or it is the other way
around. . . .' The whole question of intertextuality is
summed up in Adso's subsequent observations:

> Until then I had thought each book spoke of other
> things, human and divine, that lie outside books. Now
> I realised that, not infrequently, books speak of books;
> it is as if they spoke among themselves. In the light of
> this reflection the library seemed all the more disturbing
> to me. It was the place of a long centuries-old murmur-
> ing, an imperceptible dialogue between one parchment
> and another.[1]

Even though Jane Austen might seem the most self-sufficient of English novelists, drawing upon nothing more than her own observation of life, the insistent 'murmuring' of other books is difficult to ignore when we take a close look at her work. The 'imperciptible dialogue' between her novels and the books she has read or that her characters are reading provides a fairly continuous subtext. The books and authors referred to are often made to serve somewhat oblique functions of qualified corroboration and subversion. Jane Austen's attitude towards them ranges over the whole spectrum between genuine admiration and downright debunking, but most of the time steers clear of any univocal certainty, so that a variety of interpretations becomes possible.

At the simplest level her fictional characters are judged by their attitudes to books or by the actual texts they read or misread. Those, such as John Thorpe, who pretend to be readers but actually read nothing are of course worse than those who make no such claim, but, among those who read, not all are equally privileged. There is the classic case of Sir Edward in *Sanditon*, whose character has been warped by reading too many sentimental works:

> His fancy had been early caught by all the impassioned and most exceptionable parts of Richardson; and such authors as have since appeared to tread in Richardson's steps, so far as man's determined pursuit of woman in defiance of every feeling and convenience is concerned, had since occupied the greater part of his literary hours and formed his character ...   (ch. 8)

Women whose heads had been turned by reading have begun to appear as characters in fiction by Jane Austen's time, – for example in *The Female Quixote* by Charlotte Lennox and *The Elegant Enthusiast* by William Beckford – but Sir Edward may be the solitary male case of this malaise. The other adverse effect of books can be seen in their power to insulate human beings from the urgency and immediacy of life. Mr Bennet, who shuts himself in a library to avoid discharging his responsibilities as a father and a landlord, and Mary Bennet, who has read so many books that she can turn any real-life situation into a moralising cliché, are reminders of how books can erect barriers to shut out reality. It is this barrier that Catherine Morland has to demolish before she can come to terms with life.

But by and large Jane Austen depicts reading as a positive act. In *Sense and Sensibility* the suffering of the two heroines is aggravated by the fact that they are surrounded by a crowd of mediocre, mindless people, who have no use for books or introspection. Because Elinor and Marianne read books, Lady Middleton 'fancied them satirical, perhaps without knowing what it was to be satirical' (ch. 23). Novels and poetry generally serve to heighten the perceptions of Jane Austen's heroines, though Catherine Morland has to learn to distinguish between fiction and life. Marianne Dashwood 'had the knack of finding her way in every house to the library.' Fanny Price had been a collector of books 'from the first hour of commanding a shilling.' Anne Elliot can discuss the merits of Byron and Scott with Captain Benwick.

Emma Woodhouse, even though she cannot get around to reading the books that she thinks she ought to read, has been influenced by certain kinds of novel to create for herself an alternative world governed by a fictional code. Mr Knightley is impressed by the reading-list that Emma drew up at the age of fourteen, but during the year covered by the novel the grown-up Emma is never seen to be reading anything. The kind of reading that Emma may have encouraged in her protégée can be seen in the apologetic tone with which Harriet describes Robert Martin's obvious gaps in reading: 'He never read the "Romance of the Forest" nor the "Children of the Abbey". He had never heard of such books before I mentioned them, but he is determined to get them now as soon as he ever can' (*Emma*, ch. 4). *Children of the Abbey*, written by Regina Maria Roche and published in 1796, was one of the most popular books of the time, running through more than eleven editions and remaining in print for decades.[2] Actually the author's valuation of Robert Martin is seen nowhere more clearly than in this passage, which tells us not only that the young farmer has not developed a taste for cheap popular fiction, but also that he keeps up to date in his profession by reading agricultural reports, that he has found time to go through *The Vicar of Wakefield*, and that he reads aloud from *Elegant Extracts* to his family – much more reading than any other character in the novel is known to do.

In *Pride and Prejudice* the question of books and reading is treated more equivocally. It is not the heroine but her somewhat ludicrous sister Mary who is the most avid reader in the Bennet family. Elizabeth too is presumably not averse to reading, because we see her incurring the annoyance of Mrs Bingley for preferring books to a card game; elsewhere she reacts to Lady Catherine's interrogation about their education by defiantly defending the way they were brought up: 'We were encouraged to read ' (ch. 29). But Elizabeth also tries her best to avoid being typecast as a bookish woman. She contradicts Miss Bingley's accusation that she is a great reader and refuses to discuss books with Darcy at a dance even when urged to do so:

'What think you of books?' said he, smiling.

'Books – oh! no. I am sure we never read the same or not with the same feeling.'

'I am sorry you think so; but if that be the case, there can at least be no want of subject. We may compare our different opinions.'

'No I cannot talk of books in a ball-room . . .'

(ch. 18)

Elizabeth's disagreement with Darcy about the definition of a truly accomplished woman also hinges on the crucial question of reading. Darcy demands that such a woman, besides being an adept in drawing-room arts like singing, dancing and screen-painting, should also be a voracious reader. Elizabeth reacts sharply to this impossibly high expectation: 'I never saw such a woman, I never saw such capacity and taste and application and elegance as you describe, united' (ch. 8). While this is obviously Jane Austen's dig at the perfect heroines of popular fiction, here Elizabeth could also be protesting against Darcy's apparent inclusion of reading among the drawing-room arts. This might also explain her reluctance to talk of books in the ballroom, in casual conversation to fill in the gaps in a public ritual. Whatever her complex reasons for doing so, Elizabeth does occasionally try to disassociate herself from books and reading.

It is well-known that Jane Austen herself was an eager and unashamed reader of novels. Her letters mention scores of books – not only by well-known writers such as Richardson, Fanny Burney and Maria Edgeworth, but also by many lesser writers, including Mrs Syke, author of the five-volume gothic series *Marginana* or *Widdington Towers*, and Lady Morgan, who wrote under the pseudonym Sydney Owenson novels such as *Ida Athens* and *The Wild Irish Girl*. It was books of this type that provided the staple diet of young girls like Isabella Thorpe and Catherine Morland.[3] That Jane Austen was capable of laughing at the novels she herself read with relish is seen in *Northanger Abbey*, where the defence of the novel in the famous fifth chapter is undercut in the succeeding chapter by an exchange between two giddy girls about their favourite reading:

'. . . But my dearest Catherine what have you been doing

with yourself all this morning? Have you gone on with Udolpho?'

'Yes I have been reading it ever since I woke; and I am got to the black veil.'

'Are you indeed? How delightful! Oh! I would not tell you what is behind the black veil for the world! Are you not wild to know?!

'Oh! Yes quite; what can it be? But do not tell me: I would not be told upon any account. I know it must be a skeleton; I am sure it is Lawrentina's skeleton. Oh! I am delighted with the book! I should like to spend my whole life in reading it, I assure you; if it had not been to meet you, I would not have come away from it for all the world.'

'Dear creature, how much I am obliged to you: and when you have finished *Udolpho*, we will read the *Italian* together; and I have made out a list of ten or twelve more of the same kind for you.'

'Have you indeed? How glad I am! what are they all?'

'I will read you their names directly; Here they are in my pocket book. *Castle of Wolfenbach, Clermont, Mysterious Warnings, Necromancer of the Black Forest, Midnight Bell, Orphan of the Rhine* and *Horrid Mysteries*. Those will last us some time.'

'Yes; pretty well; but are they all horrid? are you sure they are all horrid?' (ch. 6)

The tongue-in-cheek relationship between the defence of the 'genius, wit and taste' of the maligned company of novelists in chapter 5 and the gushing sensationalism of the conversation in chapter 6 is typical of the double-edged mirth of *Northanger Abbey*. Not all the novels written or read in Jane Austen's time can have displayed 'the most thorough knowledge of human nature, the happiest delineation of its varieties, the liveliest effusions of wit and humour' (ch. 5), but, as someone involved in the enterprise of writing and reading novels, Jand Austen had no patience with those who affected to despise them. In a letter of 1798 she scoffed at a librarian who, presumably in an attempt to confer respectability on her library, announced that it would stock every branch of literature, not just novels: 'She might have spared the pretension to *our* family, who are great Novel readers and not ashamed of being so.'[4] This is not to say that Jane Austen read only novels: among other headings mentioned in her letters are books of poetry ('I have read *The Corsair*, mended my petticoat and have nothing else to do'), biographies, memoirs, travel books and even a book on military policy.

In view of all this evidence of her own voracious reading it is a little puzzling that she should feel the need to parody a girl who likes to read – Mary Bennet – unless this be the indication of some anxiety about her own image. We remember how Elizabeth hastened to correct the impression that she was a bookish woman by declaring, 'I am not a great reader and I have pleasure in many things' (*Pride and Prejudice*, ch. 8). Mary on the other hand has no pleasure in anything else. When she hears about the fun Lydia has been having she takes a sour-grapes view of all social entertainment: 'Far be it from me, my dear sister, to depreciate such pleasures. They would doubtless be congenial with the generality of female minds. But I confess it would have no charms for *me*. I should infinitely prefer a book' (ch. 39).

Sense and Sensibility is usually seen as a dialogic text where emotional restraint and self-indulgence are set against each other to define a norm for conduct; but a more interesting, because less obvious, balancing is achieved in *Pride and Prejudice*, where Mary and Lydia represent the two poles – Mary introverted and pedantic, Lydia brainless and frivolous. Elizabeth strikes a balance between interiority and vivacity, her lively wit being the antithesis of Mary's laboured rhetoric and her pride and poise being the opposite of Lydia's effervescent pursuit of men. The fact that Mary is presented as a plain girl who in the company of her more attractive sisters feels the need to compensate by her extra accomplishments – reading and music – confirms the stereotype of the bookish woman, distancing the author from any danger of identification.

Jane Austen rarely creates a character in her own image. Not only is she diffident about endorsing a woman who gives priority to reading, but there is no writer – not even an aspiring scribbler – among her characters. The overactive imagination of a Catherine Morland or an Emma might have been sublimated in writing, but instead Jane Austen highlights their confusion in negotiating the difference between the real world and the world of the imagination. Attrributable partly to the ironist's need for objectivity, this avoidance of writing as a legitimate female activity could also be an indication of Jane Austen's ambivalence towards her own vocation, an ambivalence that she shared with other women novelists of her time. The only nineteenth-century English writer to create a writer heroine is Elizabeth Barrett Browning. But even her Aurora Leigh, who conquers the handicap of a feminine education to become an extremely successful writer known all over Europe, eventually feels that her self-sufficient life is empty and gives up her career to find total fulfilment in marriage. This fear of success as an autonomous person is something that not only plagued nineteenth-century women writers in England, but has also affected many twentieth-century women with careers. Elaine Showalter has written about the hesitation that most women writers have felt about their profession, fearing that the 'authority of authorship' would somehow entail a loss of their essential femininity.[5] We recall that Jane Austen's name appeared on the title-pages of her books only after she died. The contemporary prejudice against any public role for a woman inhibited the writer from regarding her work as a profession. Although nearly half the novels published in the late eighteenth century were by women, Jane Austen creates a world where women can only be consumers of books, never producers.

The nature of the books consumed determines the personality of her heroines. In *Northanger Abbey*, where the burlesque framework overlaps with that of a *Bildungsroman*, Catherine Morland is shown to be 'in training for a heroine'. Her reading includes 'all such works as heroines must read to supply their memories with those quotations which are so serviceable and so soothing in the vicissitudes of their eventful lives' (ch. 1), and the list includes Shakespeare, Pope, Gray and Thompson, among others. The heroine for whose role Catherine is training herself belongs to the genre of popular romance but, as the novel progresses, 'the anxieties of common life began . . . to succeed to the alarm of romance' (ch. 28), teaching her that life has the tendency to overflow fictional boundaries. Catherine's education is best described in Tony Tanner's words: 'one of the things she has to learn is to break out of quotations as it were, and discover the complex differences (as well as the complex connections) between reading a book and reading the world'.[6] *Northanger Abbey* is in many ways a novel about novels, because books and life are here intertwined in a double relationship. On the one hand the novel traces Catherine's progress from the illusions created by fiction to the clear vision of reality and in the process paradoxically reveals that reality at times may not be too far from the gothic world of greed and cruelty; on the other hand the novel is a burlesque in which Catherine is less a real person than the heroine of a romance. Jane Austen frequently refers to her as 'my heroine', and feigns dismay when, instead of languishing lovelorn and sleepless on a couch, she eats heartily and sleeps soundly. Incidentally, the romantic image of the love-sick heroine is reiterated in *Sense and Sensibility*, where Marianne Dashwood, who 'would have thought herself very inexcusable had she been able to sleep at all the first night after parting from Willoughby' (ch. 16) fits the role perfectly. Unlike Catherine in *Northanger Abbey*, who remains full of health and cheer even when parted from Tilney in Bath, Marianne gets a headache and is 'unable to talk and unwilling to take any nourishment.'

While *Northanger Abbey* works in the parodic mode (intermittently, at least), in *Sense and Sensibility* the author's attitude to Marianne Dashwood is far from comic. The frame of reference is supplied not by books but by the cult of sensibility, which pertains to much more than literature, finding old twisted trees, dead leaves and ruins worthy of admiration, and insisting on an unrestrained show of emotions. There are very few literary references in *Sense and Sensibility*; the evocation of earlier texts in *Northanger Abbey* is insistent. Jane Austen obliquely invokes Richardson while admonishing Catherine for dreaming of a man before he is reported to have dreamt of her. The reference here is to Richardson's comment in *The Rambler* (1751) that 'the feminine role in courtship made it immoral as well as impolitic for a girl to allow herself to feel love for a suitor until he had actually asked for her hand in marriage'.[7] What Jane Austen is writing may be termed a mock novel, because even the gloomy fate of Catherine before the final peripeteia is not treated seriously: 'A heroine in a hack post-chaise is such a blow upon sentiment as no attempt at grandeur or pathos can withstand' (*Northanger Abbey*, ch. 29). The parodic attitude continues till the very last lines, where the author leaves the reader to decide whether the 'tendency of the work be altogether to recommend parental tyranny or reward filial disobedience' – both the alternatives pointing towards stereotypical tropes of romantic fiction. A few pages before the end she deviates from the normal novelistic convention of assuming the events and situations to be real, and lets us see that the book is, after all, an artifact with a physical shape: 'My readers will see in the tell-tale compression of the pages before them, that we are all hastening together to perfect felicity.' In a novel of the genre she is writing as well as mocking, no ending other than that of 'perfect felicity' can be envisaged.

This shifting relationship between life and art results in an interesting play with narrative tone. Tilney and Catherine have read the same books, but, unlike Tilney, who has the ability to see through the artifice of what he enjoys, gullible Catherine confuses the world created in the books with the world she inhabits. She has to play a double role in the novel – the innocent reader of gothic novels who inflates life with the extravagance of fiction, and the heroine of a mock-romantic novel that parodies fictional conventions of love, separation and marriage. There is considerable slippage between the two modes, *Bildungsroman* and parody, as in the following reflection by Catherine:

Charming as were all Mrs Radcliffe's works and charming even as were the works of all her imitators, it was not in them perhaps that human nature, at least in the midland countries of England, was to be looked for. Of the Alps and Pyrenees, with their pine forests and vices, they might give a faithful delineation. (ch. 25)

Though Catherine is seen here as gradually discovering the gap between books and life, the author deliberately subverts the process by showing her as naïvely identifying England with normalcy – obviously under the tutelage of Henry Tilney, who has held forth on this subject a few pages earlier ('Remember that we are English, that we are Christians'). At the beginning of the novel Tilney takes over from the author the role of the wry and amused commentator on life, but there is subsequently a shift in the ironic thrust of the narrative, because here the author's laughter is aimed at him as well. In *Northanger Abbey* the business of puncturing the emotional rhetoric of the romantic novel is carried out at various levels. A small incident such as sitting alone during a dance is made to appear momentous through the use of heightened melodramatic diction. Catherine's dejection at her anticlimactic return home towards the end of the novel is not given the respectful treatment a heroine's heartbreak deserves. Her mother cursorily advises her to read in *The Mirror* 'about young girls that have been spoilt for home by great acquaintances' so that Catherine can get rid of her sulking airs. When the hero and heroine finally unite at the end, this is not the triumph of ecstatic mutual passion, or of the man's undying love for the woman, but something so prosaic as to reverse all romantic expectation:

> I must confess that his affection originated in nothing better than gratitude, or in other words persuasion of her partiality for him had been the only cause of giving her a serious thought. It is a new circumstance in romance I acknowledge, and dreadfully derogatory of a heroine's dignity, but if it be as new in common life, the credit of wild imagination will at least be all my own. (ch. 30)

The shift from romance to realism suits Jane Austen's inverted ironic mode. From the spirited defence of the novel in the early part till the happy ending, *Northanger Abbey* contains numerous direct, oblique and concealed arguments about the complex relationship between life and art, making it the most self-reflexive of Jane Austen's novels.

It may be noted in passing that the conventional correlation between love and poetry is inverted in more than one context in Jane Austen's novels. While some may think of poetry as the food of love, Elizabeth Bennet is sure that it is effective in driving away love, particularly of the feeble sort: 'I am convinced that one good sonnet will starve it entirely away' (*Pride and Prejudice*, ch. 9). In *Persuasion*, Benwick, the young man who has lost his fiancée, is 'so intimately acquainted with the tenderest songs of one poet, and all the impassioned descriptions of hopeless agony of the other; he repeated with such tremulous feeling the various lines which imaged a broken heart' (ch. 11) that it seems that the self-indulgence must eventually cure the grief. Anne's prescription of 'a larger allowance of prose in his daily study', if heeded, might have produced a different result, but by the end of the novel we find him 'reading verses; or whispering' to another woman, obviously cured of the earlier love.

After exchanging preferences with Benwick about *Marmion*, *The Lady of the Lake*, *The Giaour* and *The Bride of Abydos*, Anne Elliot advises him to read prose, but she herself is no less avid a reader of poetry. She enjoys her autumn walk in Lyme Regis all the more for recalling and repeating to herself lines on the season by different poets. But poetry is also a convenient means of shutting out the painful reality of Wentworth's attentions to Louisa. Anne 'occupied her mind as much as possible in such like musings and quotations', but she cannot help overhearing snatches of their conversation, and these agitate her so much that she 'could not immediately fall into a quotation again' (*Persuasion*, ch. 10). Here quotations are desperate devices to distract the heroine's mind. In other novels they have the unintended effect of destroying spontaneity. Catherine Morland in *Northanger Abbey* so stuffs her mind with elegant extracts (ch. 2) that she erects a barrier between her perception and reality. Part of the problem of Sir Edward in *Sanditon*, who models himself on Richardson's Lovelace, is that he tends to speak in quotations. Charlotte is almost taken in by his effusion about the sea: 'she could not but think of him as a man of feeling – till he began to stagger her with the number of his quotations' (ch. 7). But books are at best a poor substitute for real feeling. In *Mansfield Park* Edmund invades the calm of Fanny's East Room where, surrounded by plants, pictures and books, she has created an oasis of peace, and shatters her by revealing his attachment to Mary Crawford. He assumes, perhaps for his own convenience, that Fanny cares only for higher pleasures such as reading – there is a book on China on the table and Crabbe's *Tales* and *The Idler* – and so will have no strong feelings about his news: 'I will not interrupt you any longer. You want to be reading.' But after Edmund has left her, disturbing her tranquillity, 'there was no reading, no China, no composure for Fanny' (ch. 16). Literature proves an inadequate cure for the blow life has dealt her.

Jane Austen is not ambivalent about books – only about the various purposes they serve in human lives. As a means of obscuring reality and stultifying experience, or of deepening apprehension of the real world, literature is of considerable concern to her. Her men and women are often known by the books they read. The moderation and commonsense that the Morland family in *Northanger Abbey* seem to embody is exemplified in Mrs Morland's preference for *Sir Charles Grandison*, a book that Jane Austen herself liked so much that she attempted a dramatic version. An ability to quote from Cowper, another of Jane Austen's favourites, is certainly a positive trait in the heroine of *Mansfield Park*. While returning from Portsmouth to Mansfield Park, Fanny's 'eagerness, her impatience, her longing . . . were such as to bring a line or two of Cowper's

Tirocinium for ever before her. "With what intense desire she wants her home" was continually on her tongue' (ch. 45).

Marianne Dashwood too is an admirer of Cowper – strong evidence against the argument that *Sense and Sensibility* is a straight moral dialectic in which Elinor has all Jane Austen's sympathy and Marianne only censure. There is no questioning the passionate sincerity of Marianne's response to literature, art or nature; she is the only true romantic in Jane Austen's novels, the only radical challenger of social conventions. She is an enthusiastic reader of Thompson, Cowper and Scott and possibly lukewarm in her response to Pope. She is disappointed when Edward Ferrar reads Cowper aloud without animation: 'To hear these beautiful lines which have frequently almost driven me wild, pronounced with such impenetrable calmness, such dreadful indifference!' (ch. 3). Her mother tries to defend Edward by pointing out that he would have done more justice to 'simple and elegant prose . . . but you would give him Cowper' (ch. 3). Marianne's passionate and absurd declaration that she could never fall in love with a person unless his literary taste exactly coincided with hers becomes the basis for Elinor's teasing comments on her relationship with Willoughby. Elinor remarks on their rapid growth of intimacy based on their trading of preferences in books: 'for *one* morning I think you have done pretty well. You know what he thinks of Cowper and Scott; you are certain of his estimating their beauties as he ought, and you have received every assurance of his admiring Pope no more than is proper' (ch. 10). In other words, Marianne has to be completely convinced of his romantic affinities for further growth of their relationship. Since Willoughby is one of those smooth and charming men in Jane Austen whose sincerity is always suspect, in spite of his reading *Hamlet* with Marianne we do not know about his actual literary or aesthetic taste. Edward Ferrars on the other hand is fairly consistent in his refusal to admire 'an old twisted tree' and the dirt lanes in the countryside and remains a steadfastly unromantic person. Marianne as usual goes too far in her insistence that all hearts should be worn on sleeves and people should constantly express a 'rapturous delight' as proof of their literary sensibility. As some other characters in Jane Austen show, it is not always easy to distinguish between feigned and spontaneous rapture, or between true intensity of feeling and mere sensationalism. When Sir Edward in *Sanditon* proclaims his preference in novels for 'the sublimities of intense feeling – such as exhibit the progress of strong passion from the first germ of incipient susceptibility to the utmost energies of reason half-dethroned' (ch. 7), he is only a caricature of the cult of sensibility that Marianne sincerely upholds.

Novels and poetry are mentioned by Jane Austen far more frequently than drama, a genre which takes centre stage only in *Mansfield Park*. Apart from the well-known episode about the staging of *Lovers' Vows*, there is the crucial chapter where Henry Crawford reads from Shakespeare's *Henry VIII* so effectively that even a reluctant Fanny is moved by the performance, if not by the performer. Reading aloud was a family pastime and Fanny had been used to good reading, but 'in Mr Crawford's reading was a variety of excellence beyond what she had ever met with' (ch. 34). The fact that Henry can illuminate equally the characters of the King, the Queen, Buckingham, Wolsey and Cromwell by his different ways of reading not only highlights his skill as an actor but goes back to the whole question about the ethics of role-playing, which first came to the surface when the young people in Mansfield Park decided to stage a play. Fanny herself is divided on the question, because, while she initially resisted involvement in the amateur theatricals, Henry Crawford's reading shows that she cannot resist the pleasure that a play, well acted, can offer. As Henry reads on, she so loses herself in her enjoyment that her needlework falls from her hand (an image of absorption repeated in *Persuasion* when the pen falls from the hand of Captain Wentworth). We find out that Crawford's ease with Shakespeare comes not from any familiarity with the text – 'I do not think I have had a volume of Shakespeare in my hand before, since I was fifteen' – but from a consummate skill in slipping smoothly into any role. Before the rehearsals began, Henry Crawford, impatient to act, had said that he could undertake to act 'any character that ever was written, from Shylock to Richard III down to the singing hero of a farce in his scarlet coat and cocked hat. I feel I could be anything or every thing' (ch. 13). The fluidity of self that allows this is certainly a dubious value in the moral world of this novel. The Crawfords' skill at acting makes them less deserving of Fanny's approval. The characters with overt charm and glibness of manner who can slide in and out of roles are morally suspect in Jane Austen's other novels too, possibly indicating an underlying anxiety about the seductive power of artificial human conduct.

Jane Austen's most sustained reference to drama occurs in *Mansfield Park*, where the episode about the enactment of *Lovers' Vows* stretches over nearly six chapters (13–18). Fanny's dissociation of herself from the enterprise cannot be a simple and direct reflection of Jane Austen's moral position. Since amateur theatricals were considered legitimate entertainment in Jane Austen's own family, the puritan stand taken in this novel needs some explanation. It was supposed at one time that Jane Austen's objection was not really to the staging of a play as such, but to the play chosen, because of Kotzebue's radical ideas and Jacobin politics. But the popularity of the play among the fashionable Tory gentry of Bath and London, who were by no means Jacobin sympathisers (even Rushworth has

seen the play in London), renders this explanation inadequate. Besides, people such as Wordsworth with strong
radical views condemned the sensationalism of certain
kinds of German play, possibly including *Lovers' Vows*.
Margaret Kirkham argues that it is not the politics of Kotzebue but the silliness and falsity of his general treatment
of human life, and, more specifically, his treatment of
women, that Jane Austen reacted against: 'He [Kotzebue]
does not depict them [women] as full human beings accoun-
table for their own actions, but as relative creatures whose
highest moral function is to excite compassion in men'.[8]
Whether Jane Austen's particular objection is to Kotzebue's depiction of women or not, she is certainly making
an ironic comment here on the taste of the young people
assembled at Mansfield Park, who reject Shakespeare and
Sheridan in favour of *Lovers' Vows*.

That the popularity of German plays in England had
begun to provoke a public reaction against them can be
surmised from Edmund Bertram's sarcastic remark at the
beginning of the venture:

> If we are to act, let it be in a theatre completely filled
> up with pit, box and gallery, and let us have a play entire
> from beginning to end; so as it be a German play, no
> matter what, with a good tricking, shifting after-piece
> and a figure-dance, and a horn-pipe, and a song between
> the acts.   (ch. 13)

In Coleridge's *Biographia Literaria*, which appeared two
years after *Mansfield Park*, we find a comparable remark
about the degenerate nature of what were popularly known
as German plays on the English stage of the time.[9] Just
as the real butts of ridicule in *Northanger Abbey* are not
the novels of romance and horror, but the readers who
let such books destroy their perception and conduct, so
in the *Lovers' Vows* episode in *Mansfield Park* Jane Aus-

ten's disapproval centres on the public taste which cla-
moured for this kind of entertainment, rather than the
plays themselves. The Bertram brothers and sisters, the
Crawfords and other people associated with this venture
are part of the same indiscriminate crowd who do not rea-
lise either the irrelevance or the potential harm of such
tinsel entertainment. After all, the play deals with illegitimate sexual relationships, setting impulse and instinct
above restraint and discipline, and portrays characters who
deceive each other. This makes it a dangerous choice for
the actors: Maria, in spite of being engaged to Rushworth,
is seeking to get closer to Crawford; Julia is competing
with Maria for Crawford's attention; Mary Crawford sees
the rehearsals as an opportunity to win over Edmund; and
all of them use the play as a means of being dishonest
with each other.

August von Kotzebue was a German playwright whose
plays, in various translations and adaptations, enjoyed a
great vogue in England at the end of the eighteenth century. His *Das Kind der Liebe*, the original of *Lovers' Vows*,
was written in 1791 and translated into English several
times; one of these versions was by Elizabeth Inchbald.
Among other things, the play is about a maid seduced
and abandoned by a baron, her rich employer. Years later,
through the intervention of their illegitimate son, they are
reunited. The other marriage in the play is between the
baron's daughter and a clergyman she brazenly courts. The
dramatic text opens up opportunities for intimacy that
would not be sanctioned in real life. Maria and Crawford
as mother and son enact a relationship that permits physical
contact without social censure, and Mary Crawford's real-
life attempts to captivate Edmund receive dramatic legitimacy during the rehearsals. The general familiarity and
the atmosphere of physical and emotional closeness that
rehearsals usually engender gives the young people the
chance to enter into relationships without commitment.

Fanny's refusal to be part of this group does not merely show her shyness and fear of public exposure, but is indicative also of her moral unease. She knows, as the others do, that the enterprise in some ways violates the authority of the absent master of Mansfield Park. She also seems to have some unarticulated reservation about impersonation and experimenting with other selves. The other persons in the group never worry about this. Tom Bertram says, 'I can conceive of no greater harm or danger in conversing in the elegant written language of some respectable author than in chattering in words of our own' (ch. 13). To him there is not much difference between being himself and playing another person because he has no definite sense of self. Initially Edmund shares Fanny's reservations, and, when asked by Mary Crawford to take the part of the clergyman because it will correspond to his future role in life, he retorts, 'The man who chooses the profession itself is perhaps one of the last who would wish to represent it on the stage.' He also feels – somewhat priggishly – that acting requires the kind of abandon that is difficult for 'gentlemen and ladies, who have all the advantages of education and decorum to struggle through'.

Fanny's theoretical objection to play-acting is further strengthened when she reads the play. Tony Tanner, in discussing the *Lovers' Vows* episode in *Mansfield Park*, has referred to the old Platonic objection that the imitation of a base character will have a demoralising influence on the person. Fanny's views are not so well formulated, but her instinctive disapproval is strong enough to withstand the efforts of the entire group to counter it. There are times when she feels lonely and left out, but her occasional longing to be included in the charmed circle dissolves when she sees the schemes and duplicity implicit in the project. Fanny is firm even when Edmund succumbs to the lure of vicarious life. Edmund is embarrassed about the 'appearance' of inconstancy that his acting will give after

he has so strongly objected to the project, and even afterwards he remains caught 'between his theatrical and his
real part'. Fanny remains the only figure who can perceive
the reality behind the appearance. Earlier, in the garden
at Sotherton, she was the only person who stayed put while
her companions threaded the serpentine pathways, and
as a result she gained an overall view of their various
manoeuvres. The *Lovers' Vows* episode provides a parallel
design: the others rehearse their real and dramatic parts
with her, and she is the only one who can understand their
real motives. Julia's anger at being rejected, Rushworth's
anxiety about Crawford's charm, Mary's schemes for win-
ning Edmund, and Edmund's own concealed desires all
converge upon Fanny; all the actors gravitate towards her,
because she occupies an inviolate space and offers them
a safe repository for their feelings. But it should also be
pointed out that the pressures on Fanny keep mounting,
and even she might have been dislodged from her well-
defined neutrality if Sir Thomas had not suddenly returned
home.

A play thus serves a different purpose in Jane Austen's
novels from other kinds of literary texts. Fanny is happy
with her books and plants in the East Room because they
offer her a sanctuary and protect her from the assaults
of the outside world, which might threaten her sense of
self. The performance of a play, on the other hand, is
a public act where social conventions and ethical values
come into play. Therefore the self-reflexivity and playful
ambiguity that mark Jane Austen's references to novels
and poetry do not extend to drama. As a social event,
a theatrical performance has to be seen in the larger context
of the community and its normative codes.

6 'Speak well enough to be unintelligible'

> ... 'I understand you perfectly well.'
>
> 'Me? Yes, I cannot speak well enough to be unintelligible.'
>
> 'Bravo! an excellent satire on modern language.'
>
> *Northanger Abbey*

When Jane Austen expressly warned her niece Anna against the use of the phrase 'vortex of dissipation' in her novel, she was evidently making some playful distinction between the ethics of human behaviour and the aesthetics of language use: 'I do not object to the thing, but I cannot bear the expression; it is such thorough novel slang – and so old, that I dare say Adam met with it in the first novel he opened.'[1] But the concerns in her own novels, both with language and with human conduct, repeatedly make such a distinction untenable, because lexical precision in her system of values is usually a positive moral index pointing towards clarity of perception – and possibly even integrity of character. Naming confers reality upon objects; and even states of mind until exactly verbalised can remain fluid and indeterminate. Lazily verbalised, they not only become imprecise but are also transformed and falsified. Marianne Dashwood in *Sense and Sensibility*, who is particularly fastidious about keeping language unsullied by ossified words, declares, 'Sometimes I have kept my feelings to myself because I could find no language to describe them but what was worn and hackneyed out of all sense and meaning' (ch. 18).

Herein lies a paradox in Jane Austen, who puts such a high premium on the social dimension of human life. Language after all is a social code whose effectiveness depends on the users' familiarity with its conventions. Yet at some point the familiarity, instead of facilitating communication, begins to act as a barrier. Like her favoured fictional characters, Jane Austen is conscious of this transition of meaning into meaninglessness. Mrs Gardiner curbs Elizabeth's enthusiasm by commenting, 'But that expression of "violently in love" is so hackneyed, so doubtful, so indefinite, that it gives me very little idea' (*Pride and Prejudice*, ch. 25).

Careless use of language in most cases arises out of some other lapse which lies below the surface. Taking offence at Sir John Middleton's raillery that she is 'setting her cap' at Willoughby, Marianne Dashwood delivers a lecture on language, but her annoyance arises as much from the mindless use of clichés as from the gender assumptions underlying all such social banter. She reprimands him,

> That is an expression, Sir John, which I particularly dislike. I abhor every common-place phrase by which wit is intended; and 'setting one's cap at a man', or 'making a conquest' are the most odious of all. Their tendency is gross and illiberal; and if their construction could ever be deemed clever, time has long ago destroyed all its ingenuity. (*Sense and Sensibility*, ch. 9)

Bad wit and doubtful morality combine to irritate Marianne Dashwood, but, as most women know, to counter a sexist joke with rational argument is more difficult than catching a man out on other grounds. Marianne thus turns her objections into a homily on the misuse of language.

A few minutes earlier, her mother had chided Sir John for using the verb 'catch' to describe her daughters' attitude to men in general and to one man in particular. Gently but firmly, she had assured him that Mr Willoughby would not be inconvenienced 'by the attempts of either of my daughters towards what you call *catching him*. It is not an employment to which they had been brought up.'

The social discourse of the time was strewn with such invisible metaphors that portrayed women as predators who must trick moneyed men into marriage, using their beauty as bait. Until they succeeded in doing so, they were supposed to remain liabilities to their families. Much of the conversation recorded in Jane Austen's novels tacitly accepts this outlook. John Dashwood is much concerned about his sister's illness and loss of her bloom: 'I question whether Marianne *now* would marry a man worth more than five or six hundred a year at the utmost' (ch. 33). Whether it is Mrs Jennings boasting about her good luck in getting her daughters 'off her hand' or John Dashwood urging his sister to *try harder* for Colonel Brandon – 'A very little trouble on your side secures him' – it is the imperceptible connotations of profit and loss, hunt and chase, that construct the whole humiliating discourse.

Barring a few spirited characters such as Elizabeth Bennet who can use their wit against the implied degradation of their sex. Jane Austen's sensitive women suffer it in silence most of the time. In her own authorial voice, however, Jane Austen can subvert these all-too-familiar assumptions with her celebrated irony, as in the well-known sentence on the first page of *Mansfield Park*: 'The world does not have as many men of good fortune as there are pretty women to deserve them.' While pretending to accede to the implied equation in the marital market-place between men's money and women's beauty, she manages to expose its absurdity at a logical level.

Marianne Dashwood, the passionate advocate of spontaneity of behaviour and purity of expression, thinks she has found a soul-mate in Willoughby because at first 'their taste was strikingly alike. The same books, the same passages were idolized by each ... he acquiesced in all her decisions, caught all her enthusiasm ...' (*Sense and Sensibility*, ch. 10). How she is deceived can be seen in Willoughby's long confession to Elinor later in the novel. His language here is clogged with the kind of dead expressions that Marianne detests. Recapitulating an earlier occasion when he received a letter from Marianne, he says,

> My feelings were very very painful – Every line, every word was – in the hackneyed metaphor which their dear writer, were she here, would forbid – a dagger to my heart. To know that Marianne was in town – was in the same language – a thunderbolt. Thunderbolts and daggers! – What a reproof she would have given me.
>
> (ch. 44)

Willoughby's self-conscious apologetic tone about his banal language does not exonerate him; it only makes explicit the fact that he has no other way of expressing himself than in the language of bad romantic novels. Given the reciprocal relationship between language and sensibility in Jane Austen's world it is quite appropriate that the false hero Willoughby should only deal in counterfeit metaphors. The indifference to the exact relationship between the signifier and the signified amounts to a moral lacuna in this world, and the language used by Willoughby in his confession, though shot through with self-conscious mockery directed towards himself, rules out the possibility of his ever being totally reinstated in the reader's estimation.

The language of letters is even more revealing evidence of a person's character than speech because it is more carefully and deliberately constructed. That Robert Martin can write a concise letter proposing marriage to Harriet in language which 'though plain was strong and unaffected' is meant to dispose the reader in his favour (*Emma*, ch. 7), and that Frank Churchill should write an intense, high-pitched letter 3000 words long without the relief of a single paragraph break (ch. 50) can only weigh against him, even though in the generosity of the happy ending everybody tends to be forgiven. This composition, however, is subjected to critical scrutiny by Knightley, who joins Emma in reviewing and dissecting at length a communication that is intended for neither of them. Despite Tilney's insistence that women are more prolific letter-writers than men, we find in Jane Austen's novels that men tend to write longer letters than women. Close in length to Frank Churchill's explanatory letter is the one justifying his conduct that Darcy pushes into Elizabeth's hand in the park at Rosings. These letters of retrospective clarification are perhaps used more as narrative devices than strategies of characterisation – unlike, for example, Mr Collins' letter in *Pride and Prejudice*, which precedes his appearance and helps to define and individualise him. The moral value of good writing is always emphasised – even in incidental remarks such as those of Edward Ferrar on a letter from Lucy Steele, whom, he is relieved to find, he does not have to marry after all: 'In a sister it is bad enough, but in a wife! How I have blushed over the pages of her writing' (*Sense and Sensibility*, ch. 49).

There are, however, some occasions when letters do not match the personality of the writers. Take for example Captain Wentworth's brief and passionate letter which clinches the issue at the end of *Persuasion*. The urgent and impulsive language can hardly be associated with the taciturn hero we have encountered so far, but this letter has to be seen in the context in which it is written – the recipient standing in the same room engaged in a dialogue meant to be overheard, in which he must intervene. The letter is part of a larger dramatic action in a public room where a number of conversations are going on simultaneously. At the time of writing the writer's feelings are in a ferment, his intention still unformed. The abrupt sentences and the tumbling-forth of short bursts of emotion may be the result of the very extraordinary circumstances of composition. Jane Austen's heroes generally tend to be sober and circumspect, with total command over themselves. The uncharacteristic intensity of Wentworth's language here can be explained in yet another way. It has often been pointed out that *Persuasion* was written at a time when Jane Austen's own views on spontaneity and restraint, sense and sensibility, emotion and decorum were in a state of transition. While some of her earlier characters learn to be prudent through experience, Anne Elliot makes the reverse journey: 'She had been forced into prudence in her youth, she learnt romance as she grew older ...' (*Persuasion*, ch. 4). Wentworth's change from cautious reserve to unrestrained confession may be part of the same process.

In any case the letter in question comes at a point in the novel when Jane Austen is faced with a particularly knotty problem of narrative closure. The impasse had to be resolved without any help from external events. In a society that strictly limited the circumstances in which women could write letters to men outside the family, Jane Austen had to somehow make her heroine take the initiative in effecting the final reconciliation. After making one wrong choice, she finally was able to make Anne – without actually getting her to write a letter or directly confess her love to Wentworth – manage to convey her feelings through a theoretical discussion about women being more constant than men – 'It is perhaps our fate rather than our merit' – unsettling him enough to drop all his guards and his pen (ch. 23). Jane Austen's earlier scrupulous concern with language as a moral metaphor seems to be have been abandoned in her last novel, either by choice or of necessity.

But generally in Jane Austen recognition of the power of language and the careful use of it indicate true sensibility. Nowhere is this more apparent than in *Northanger Abbey*. Not only does the hero have a lexicographer's scrupulous concern for words, but the author carries on a continuous literary game in which the vocabulary of romance is made to interact with comic-realistic language describing the growth of an ordinary girl, with occasional superimpositions of the rhetoric of the gothic mode. The innocent heroine also provides the author with a pretext for ironic observation on fashionable society, through the familiar eighteenth-century device of using a foreigner or outsider to highlight or expose society's follies.[2] Catherine Morland's sad confession 'I cannot speak well enough to be unintelligible' becomes Jane Austen's indictment of sophisticated verbal exchanges in which language is used to obfuscate rather than to communicate. Catherine is artless enough to say exactly what she feels and even praise a young man's dancing without knowing that she has transgressed a code. With her naïve lack of indirection she continues to be baffled by the paradox of polite speech: 'but why should he say one thing so positively and mean another all the while, was most unaccountable. How were people, at that rate, to be understood?' (ch. 26). She learns only very gradually that people do not always want to be understood and that language may serve as a sophisticated means of concealing thoughts. By the time she receives Isabella's insincere letter declaring eternal love for her brother and friendship for herself, Catherine has learnt to see through false words and feigned emotion (ch. 27). But Isabella's letter is so blatantly false and so outrageously affected that it may not be fair to Catherine to consider her recognition of its hypocrisy a measure of the advance in her education. The insistent hyperbole and superlatives ('greatest coxcomb', 'amazingly disagreeable', 'you are dearer to me than anybody I can conceive'), the contradictions and shallowness ('he is the only man I ever did or could love, and I trust you will convince him of it. The spring fashions are partly down and the hats are the most frightful you can imagine'; 'I wear nothing but purple now; I know I look hideous in it; but no matter; it is your dear brother's favourite colour') turn it into a parody of affected hypocritical communication rather than a realistic sample of the genre. Since comic exaggeration is the narrative norm in *Northanger Abbey*, these passages fit in with the prevailing mood of playfulness. When the high-pitched notes of a giddy character are replaced by the author's voice, a balanced and judicious rhetoric conceals the exaggeration, heightening the comic effect through contrast:

> The advantages of natural folly in a beautiful girl have been already set forth by the capital pen of a sister author; and to her treatment of the subject I will only add, in justice to men, that though, to the larger and more trifling part of the sex, imbecility in females is a great enhancement of their personal charms, there is a portion of them too reasonable and too well-informed themselves, to deserve anything more in women then ignorance.   (Ch. 14)

Wedged into the comic discrepancy between the formality of the language and the mocking irreverence of the content are Jane Austen's incisive comments on the popular fiction of the time that idealised silly heroines and on the social norms that made intelligence a definite liability in women.

Catherine Morland is Jane Austen's only 'ignorant' heroine; all the others, possibly with the interesting exception of Emma Woodhouse, are distinguished by their control over language and therefore over their perception of reality right from the beginning. Even Catherine Morland's potential is clearly indicated at the outset. Though she may not know about the concept of 'the picturesque' or the benefits of studying history, and though she may even occasionally use words in an imprecise manner, she is never gushing or loquacious – the two hallmarks of Jane Austen's stupid women. Infected by the speech fashions of Bath, she once uses the word 'amazingly' in the current superlative sense, but is immediately censured by Tilney. Careful to guard Catherine against romantic profligacy, Tilney also criticises her use of the phrase 'promised faithfully', pointing to its illogicality: 'A faithful promise! that puzzles me. I have heard of a faithful performance, but a faithful promise – the fidelity of promising!' (ch. 24). This must have been a common misuse at the time, because Lydia in *Pride and Prejudice* mentions a secret she 'promised . . . so faithfully to keep' (ch. 51). Tilney's sensitivity to language is very close to the author's own. As soon as he appears in *Northanger Abbey* he takes over the burden of ironic commentary from the author as well as her verbal and lexical concerns. His backhanded compliment on women's epistolary skill echoes Jane Austen's own attitude towards a breathless, frothy, supposedly feminine style of letter-writing: 'The usual style of letter writing among women is faultless except in three particulars – . . . A general deficiency of subject, a total inattention to stops, and a very frequent ignorance of grammar' (ch. 3). After this initial exaggeration to tease Catherine, Tilney quickly withdraws the sexist bias in the stricture by admitting, 'In every power of which taste is the foundation, excellence is pretty fairly divided between the sexes.' His obsession with language, however, persists through the novel, and he is generally remembered as the Jane Austen character who delivered the famous polemic on verbal precision so often quoted by teachers of writing even today:

and this is a very nice day; and we are taking a very

nice walk; and you two are very nice ladies. Oh! it is
a very nice word indeed! It does for everything. Originally, perhaps it was applied only to express neatness,
propriety, delicacy, or refinement; people were nice in
their dress, in their sentiments, or their choice. But now
every commendation on every subject is composed in
that one word.   (ch. 14)

A good pupil, Catherine, who could hardly maintain 'the
language of tolerable calmness' on first hearing the word
'abbey', learns under Tilney's tutelage how to control both
her language and her imagination.

The criss-crossing of the realistic and the romance mode
in this novel is effected more through switching tone than
through the use of two sets of lexical items, but occasional
instances of the latter ('baronet's son'/'foundling'; 'sleepless couch'/'pillow strewn with thorn and wet with tears')
keep the double frame visible. From time to time Catherine
is described as 'our heroine', and, in case her unromantic
fate pushes the parodic intent to the background by attracting sympathy, it is reinforced towards the end with some
deliberation:

A heroine returning at the close of her career, to her
native village, in all the triumph of recovered reputation,
and all the dignity of a countess, with a long train of
noble relations in their several phaetons, and three waiting maids in a travelling chaise-and-four behind her is
an event on which the pen of the contriver might well
delight to dwell ... But my affair is wholly diferent.
(ch. 29)

The gothic interventions also happen at regular intervals.
Words such as 'shocking', 'dreadful', 'horrid', 'murder' and
'blood' frighten Eleanor Tilney until she discovers that
their referents are safely contained within 'three duo-

decimo volumes, two hundred and seventy-six pages in each, with a frontispiece to the first, of the tombstones and a lantern' (ch. 14). Such vocabulary surfaces again during Catherine's journey to Northanger Abbey, when Tilney scares her by conjuring up visions of 'gloomy chambers', a 'broken lute', an 'extinguished lamp', a 'violent storm'. 'Peals of thunder', a 'dagger', 'drops of blood', and so on (ch. 20). In fact Catherine's experience upon arrival at the Abbey turns out to be most ordinary. Every windowpane here is 'so large, so clear, so light', and the fireplace, instead of 'ample and ponderous carving of former times', has plain slabs of marble. In her own room in the Abbey the old chest and the high, old-fashioned black cabinet bring back the mood of suspense. 'The wind roared down the chimney', 'the rain beat in torrents against the windows', 'darkness impenetrable and immovable' – the perfect setting for a horror novel. But each time this gothic mood is evoked it is subsequently dissolved at a different level of levity.

The leaps of Catherine's imagination, from her initial suspicion that the General tortured his wife to the conjecture that he kept her in the dungeon on a diet of coarse bread and finally the conviction that he murdered her, are traced in the heightened language appropriate to the genre of *The Mysteries of Udolpho*, with frequent references to family vaults, coffins, the waxen figure of a dead woman, and so forth. Eventually she undertakes a secret expedition to confirm her hypothesis, but is discovered by Tilney. A contrite Catherine then decides to banish all thoughts of terror and crime, poison and sleeping-potions, to the remote regions of 'Alps and Pyrenees with their pine forests and vice' (ch. 25). Jane Austen's double-take here makes the novel more diverting than a straightforward progress of the heroine from romantic delusion to clear-eyed perception would have been. Catherine thinks she has learnt her lesson: 'The visions of romance were over. Catherine was completely awakened. Henry's address . . . had thoroughly opened her eyes to the extravagance of her late fancies'. But her subsequent musings reveal to the reader how deluded she still is, how parochial in her understanding of human nature. The parodic intent still strong, Jane Austen, while attributing to her heroine a withdrawal from the horrors of Mrs Radcliffe's novels to the safe boundaries of the Midland counties of England, mocks the gothic novels' tendency to exploit exotic location to romantic effect:

> Italy, Switzerland and the South of France might be as fruitful in horrors as they were there represented. Catherine dared not doubt beyond her own country, and even of that, if hard-pressed, would have yielded the northern and western extremities . . . Among the Alps and Pyrenees perhaps there were no mixed characters. There such as were not as spotless as an angel, might have the disposition of a fiend. But in England it was not so; among the English, she believed, in their hearts and habits, there was a general though unequal mixture of good and bad.   (ch. 25)

Obviously, the author's amused comment here is ascribed to Catherine as a serious reflection, reminding us of the various levels of narrative play at work in the text, including the constantly shifting frames of parody, burlesque and *Bildungsroman*, all visible through the texture of language.

'With less genius for writing than Charlotte Brontë she got infinitely more said', commented Virginia Woolf on Jane Austen in *A Room of One's Own*.[3] Indeed, Jane Austen got more said because she was operating at several levels simultaneously. Take, for example, the following sentence from the first chapter of *Mansfield Park*, where Mrs Price, estranged from her sisters for eleven years through an imprudent marriage, attempts to regain their

sympathy: 'She addressed Lady Bertram in a letter which
spoke so much contrition and despondence, such a super-
fluity of children and such a want of almost everything
else, as could not but dispose them all to a reconciliation.'
The balanced construction, the adequate telescoping of
a long process into a neatly rounded-off sentence allow
the author to maintain an amused distance from both par-
ties, the supplicant and the forgiver. The well-known opening sentence of *Pride and Prejudice* demonstrates the same
act of equivocal distancing, because we know, as does the
author, that what is being stated is no truth, let alone a
universal one. The young man in question may not feel
the want, but the others around him – particularly parents
of marriageable daughters – would like him to be so
inclined. This kind of controlled and equivocal compression is made possible only by the author's extraordinary
control over her medium and her ability to remain wryly
noncommittal towards the prevailing values of society.

Jane Austen takes it for granted that precision of language is a sign of correct sensibility; that superlatives and
excesses hint at falsity, and that platitudes point to mental
vacuity. A classic example of such vacuity is provided by
Mr Collins in *Pride and Prejudice*, who can speak in no
language other than clichés, in no tone except that of pompous formality. In his famous proposal, the reasons for
his desire to marry Elizabeth are arranged in an order
guaranteed to offend: first, he is aware of his social duty
– a clergyman must marry; second, he hopes that marriage
will make him happy; third, he wishes to show his gratitude
to his patroness, who wants to see him married; fourth,
he feels a humanitarian urge to compensate the Bennet
family by marrying one of the girls whom he is depriving
of property; and lastly, a plea meant to be passionate –
he has fallen violently in love with Elizabeth. The gap
between his officious tone and the romantic vocabulary
('in the most animated language the violence of my affec-

tion') turns him into the most memorable caricature in the Jane Austen canon. The way he addresses Elizabeth may be seen as a burlesque of the way such matters were ordered in the conduct books of the time. The character of Mr Collins may even have been suggested by Mrs Hannah More's *Coeleb in Search of Wife*, a very earnest account of how a solemn and humourless clergyman of twenty-four goes around from family to family looking for the perfect wife. The search goes on for two volumes of 351 and 469 pages respectively, until he finds the paragon of virtue who answers all the requirements.

Coeleb not only has the stiffness and self-righteousness of Mr Collins but also has his dislike of fiction from the circulating library. Mrs More evidently approves her character's lament that 'novels with very few admirable exceptions had done infinite mischief by so completely establishing the omnipotence of love, that the young reader was almost systematically taught an unresisting submission to a feeling because the feeling was commonly represented as irresistible'.[4] Romantic love is obviously seen here as something constructed by fictional discourse, and the effect of this discourse on social conventions is reflected in Mr Collins' proposal to Elizabeth: his mention of love, even though as an afterthought, is a concession to the expected rhetoric on such an occasion. The words have been previously rehearsed, because, as we know, he was in the habit of 'arranging such little elegant compliments as may be adapted to ordinary occasions' (ch. 14).

If Mr Collins' language is always premeditated and pompous, Mrs Bennet's is always frothy, formless and instantaneous, bubbling over with an excess of adjectives and superlatives ('vast deal', 'greatest', 'sweetest', 'sweet', 'charming' – all crammed into four lines in chapter 9). Her sentences run on indeterminately without any definite closure (the sentence mentioned above consists of fifty-five words), because speech for her is not the expression of

clearly thought-out ideas, but a meandering monologue
with no controlling logic or punctuation. Her husband's
cryptic, understated and syntactically concise statements
constructed with carefully chosen words emphasise the
couple's incompatibility.

Language also plays a prominent role in the way the
five Bennet girls are individualised. Elizabeth, who inherits
her father's wit without his cynicism, keeps her end up
in a repartee with obvious enjoyment but without loqua-
city, and is the only one of the girls who can use words
as weapons in a vulnerable situation. A witty woman's
control of language can become a strategy for making the
best of her confining situation and a defence against total
domination by those above her in gender and economic
hierarchies. There is no evidence that any of the other
sisters chafe against their assigned roles as Elizabeth does.
Jane's bland, good-natured sentences register indiscriminate approval of everyone, and Lydia's exclamations and
outbursts never transcend the trivial. Their mother's incon-
clusive vagueness reappears in Lydia's sentences, with
their stream of clauses cobbled together with 'and' and
their litter of stock phrases and similes that Elizabeth
would shudder to use ('smiled like anything', 'Aye', 'I
declare', 'Oh Lord', 'La'). Lydia's speech comes closest
to the syntactically and typographically fragmented language of the women in popular sentimental fiction, who
must stress their 'non-verbal sensibility through emphasiz-
ing the limited nature of verbal communication'.[5] Mary's
bookish speech is meant to emphasise her second-hand
response to life, and it is little wonder that she does not
find Mr Collins' letter defective 'in point of composition'.
Kitty remains a shadowy and petulant satellite of Lydia
with very few lines of dialogue. Collectively, all Elizabeth's
sisters place in relief her controlled verbal sparkle.

Darcy too is a careful user of words and capable of a
dry wit, but in the first part of the novel he is too guarded

and caustic in his speech, completely lacking Elizabeth's verve. When Bingley chides Darcy for the artificiality of his writing-style ('He does not write with ease. he studies too much for words of four syllables' – (ch. 10), Darcy's answer – 'My stile is very different' – is meant also to emphasise the difference in character between him and his uncomplicated friend. Bingley, like Jane, is too simple a person, too easy to please, and does not seem to possess a hard core of self. A geometric relationship is set up between the malleable, fluid personalities of Jane and Bingley on the one hand, and the sharp-edged individual-ism of Darcy and Elizabeth on the other. Jane Austen sets the two extremes against each other – casual intemper-ate users of language and the cautious caustic ones – to highlight the contours of different personality types.

Silence and speech are also necessary elements by which the private and public domains are mapped out. Unlike Collins and Wickham, who in their different ways blur the distinction between the private and public spheres, Darcy and Elizabeth need to keep their personal space inviolate in a world that is eager to intrude and invade. Fiercely possessive of his privacy, Darcy refuses to play up to casual society. He avoids direct answers to all prying questions, such as Lady Catherine's 'What is that you are saying, Fitzwilliam? What is it you are talking of? What are you telling Miss Bennet? Let me hear what it is' (ch. 31). But he has the advantage of money, class and sex, which make his arrogance almost a virtue. Elizabeth has a harder task warding off probing questions. Darcy's obser-vation to her 'We neither of us perform to strangers' is meant to be a compliment, acknowledging this quality.

Those with a guarded area of privacy that cannot be encroached upon are clearly marked out – far too clearly – from the characters who, with nothing below the surface, have no need to conceal anything. Lydia Bennet, who can-not keep a confidence ('But gracious me! I quite forgot!

I ought not to have said a word about it. I promised them so faithfully ... It was to be such a secret!' – ch. 51), and Mrs Bennet, who blurts out in public all her idle daydreams, are comic cut-outs like Mr Collins and Lady Catherine – predictable in their reactions and frozen in their particular forms of speech. Wickham is not a character, but a type who appears with some modification in the other novels as Willoughby, Frank Churchill, Walter Elliot and Henry Crawford. These charming and glib young men who give the impression of openness in their speech are often diverting attention from some concealed design.

The question of concealment and candour (a word which for Jane Austen meant 'freedom from malice or unwillingness to find fault' but is here used in the contemporary sense of openness and frankness) triggers off complicated variations in the novels of Jane Austen. By setting Elinor's cautious reticence against Marianne's deliberate refusal to be anything but spontaneous, the author lets the two sisters define each other. Marianne pities her sister for not having 'that rapturous delight which in her opinion could alone be called taste' and considers it a deficiency in Elinor that she does not cry as much as Marianne herself does on quitting their home in Norland. 'Even now her self-command is invariable, when is she dejected or melancholy? When does she try to avoid society, or appear restless or dissatisfied in it?' (*Sense and Sensibility*, ch. 8). While Marianne accuses Elinor of insensitivity, Elinor is afraid for her sister, who by being so unreserved makes herself vulnerable in a world of treachery and meanness.

Keeping one's counsel is more often than not a superior moral quality in Jane Austen's world. Elinor, who refuses to wear her heart on her sleeve, proves to be a better survivor than Marianne; the quietly meditative Fanny Price and Anne Elliot, who seem encased in silence, triumph at the end; the laconic heroes Darcy and Knightley stand above the chattering lesser beings. We are supposed to think the better of Edward Ferrars for quietly resisting the currently fashionable jargon of the pituresque and retaining the understated directness of his speech: 'I shall call hills steep, which ought to be bold; surfaces strange and uncouth which ought to be irregular and rugged' (*Sense and Sensibility*, ch. 18). The endless stream of small talk in Jane Austen's novels comes from such characters as Mrs Norris, Mrs Jennings, Mrs Bennet, Miss Bates and Mrs Elton, confirming the general assumption that women love to indulge in meaningless conversation registering ephemeral details of texture and mood. Mr Knightley, when reporting an event to Emma, adds, 'Your friend Harriet will make a much longer history when you see her. She will give you all the minute particulars which only woman's language can make interesting. In our communications we deal only in the great' (*Emma*, ch. 56). The distinction here may not be between men and women, as Knightley so smugly presumes, but between two types of personality. In Jane Austen's novels reserve is meant to be linked with intelligence and an ability to feel deeply. Knightley's scorn of the smooth talker is evident in his rather inarticulate declaration of love: 'I cannot make speeches, Emma . . . if I loved you less, I might be able to talk about it more' (ch. 49).

But where does the positive virtue of reserve shade into secrecy and concealment – qualities dangerously close to treachery and deceit? A kind of self-righteousness creeps into the voice of Knightley when he reads Frank Churchill's letter revealing his secret engagement to Jane Fairfax: 'His own mind full of intrigue, that he should suspect it in others. Mystery – finesse – how they pervert the understanding! My Emma, does not everything seem to prove more and more the beauty of truth and sincerity in all our dealings with each other?' (ch. 51). Emma squarely blames Frank Churchill for not being open and for causing her embarrassment over his deliberate double-dealing:

'What right had he to come amongst us with affection and faith engaged, and with manners so very disengaged?' (ch. 46). Neither Emma nor Knightley is an unbiased party in this case, but their anger against Frank Churchill can also be explained by the fact that, unlike Jane Fairfax, who only withheld the truth by maintaining silence, he actively deceived others. In the unwritten code operating in Jane Austen's novels, matters pertaining to private emotions may be inviolable in their secrecy, but those relating to the social sphere – marriage, engagement, inheritance, income – must be made public; hence the strictures against secret engagements both in *Emma* and in *Sense and Sensibility*. Emma's vision is a completely social one without hidden recesses of introspection or solitude, and that is why she feels the need to condemn the confusion caused in Highbury by Jane and Frank's concealment of their relationship.

Yet *Emma* contains a great deal of attempted concealment and game-playing, manifested in the charades, riddles, poems and puzzles that punctuate the novel. Everyone belonging to Emma's circle is 'invited to contribute any really good enigmas, charades or conundrums that they might recollect' for Harriet's riddle book, but the banality of the contributions received – a few lines of a common song from Mr Woodhouse and a clichéd love poem with tired metaphors about wealth and power composed by Mr Elton – sums up the dreary literalness of the company Emma keeps. At the ill-fated Box Hill picnic, Frank Churchill's valiant attempt to galvanise the wit of the party produces nothing better than Mr Weston's feeble conundrum on Emma's name, and Emma's cruel joke at the cost of Miss Bates. Although in actual concealment of motives, misunderstandings and manipulations of human beings *Emma* is a complex novel, the characters seem unable to transcend the literal level, singularly incapable of indulging in verbal ingenuity. During a word-game played with the children's box of letters Frank Churchill amuses himself by simultaneously involving and embarrassing the two women. But it is a cheap trick, immediately seen through by Mr Knightley: 'These letters were but the vehicle for gallantry and trick. It was a child's play, chosen to conceal a deeper game on Frank Churchill's part' (ch. 40).

Of all Jane Austen's heroines, Fancy Price is the most inarticulate: she shrinks from speech as from physical contact. Growing up as a poor relation in a rich family, she develops the natural psychological symptoms of withdrawal that eventually become her moral defence as well. What we remember of her speech after finishing the novel is largely made up of sentences of denial – refusals to act, refusals to marry. She is also the only heroine who refuses to be amused. Her cousin Edmund therefore speaks to her 'without any touch of that spirit of banter or the air of levity which [he] knew to be offensive to Fanny' (ch. 17). This solemn, silent girl stands at the centre of *Mansfield Park*, quietly listening, absorbing and evaluating. Because she is a courteous listener, she becomes the repository of everybody's confidences. At Sotherton her symbolic placement near the locked gate leading to the wilderness makes her the mute witness to the drama of hide-and-seek enacted by the Crawfords, her cousins and Mr Rushworth in their winding 'serpentine courses'. Similarly, during the rehearsal for *Lovers' Vows*, Fanny is the still point around whom the emotional intrigue brews. She is destined always to observe minutely and listen attentively. If elsewhere Jane Austen's art of characterisation depends on creating nuances of speech, in Fanny's case the character is made to grow through speechlessness. The longest utterance given to her is in chapter 32 and consists of ten lines. Driven to desperation, with her back to the wall, she has to tell her uncle that she cannot marry Henry Crawford. This uncharacteristic effort exhausts her and then she sinks into monosyllabic responses, no longer trying to convince her uncle of her reasons:

> 'Have you any reason, my child, to think ill of Mr Crawford's temper?'
> 'No, Sir.'
> She longed to add 'But of his principles I have' but her heart sank under the appalling prospect of discussion, explanation, and probably non-conviction.
>
> (ch. 32)

Fanny's flight from speech is counterpointed by the uninhibited and sprightly verbal contribution of the Crawfords to the life of Mansfield Park. While they enliven the atmosphere there, their unexpurgated high spirits occasionally threaten the decorum of the great house. Mary Crawford scandalises both Edmund and Fanny by talking irreverently about admirals, their 'bickerings and jealousies'. This was a rank in the Navy much valued and held in awe after the Napoleonic wars. But Mary quips, 'Certainly my home at my uncle's brought me acquainted with a circle of admirals. Of *Rears* and *Vices* I saw enough. Now do not be suspecting me of a pun, I entreat' (ch. 7).

Punning in Jane Austen tends to be a sign of moral ambiguity as well as verbal agility. It has been pointed out by several critics that the author's attitude towards Mary Crawford is not very simple.[6] Mary is not set against Fanny in the same straightforward way as Isabella is set against Catherine Morland in *Northanger Abbey* or Lucy Steele against Elinor Dashwood in *Sense and Sensibility*. The difference is clearly visible at the level of language. Lucy and Isabella, like Mrs Elton, are coarse and insensitive in their speech, while Mary has the advantage of sophistication and wit. Nina Auerbach has pointed out the centrality of the word 'ought' in *Mansfield Park*: '"Ought" tolls constantly, its very sound bringing a knell of absolutism, and nobody uses it with more assurance than the hero and the heroine'.[7] Part of the charm of the Crawfords is that they are outside this normative world of 'ought', merrily shocking people with their unashamed materialism, amorality and restlessness. Their constant search for amusement and love of improvement go against the conservative grain of the novel, although their presence certainly adds a sparkle to this world of solid respectability. Speechless Fanny wins her moral victory at the end, completely eliminating the witty and articulate Crawfords. Though in the last chapter of *Mansfield Park* we are told that Fanny and Edmund's 'home was the home of affection and comfort' one would no doubt miss at the parsonage of Mansfield the kind of enlivening banter that Elizabeth Bennet can be expected to bring to Pemberley. We remember that Darcy's only shortcoming in Elizabeth's eyes at the end of *Pride and Prejudice* is 'that he had yet to learn to be laughed at', a shortcoming she undoubtedly will hasten to remedy.

Jane Austen's characters speak in a number of different registers but with few exceptions they all more or less speak the language of the genteel upper middle class at the end of the eighteenth century. The lower rungs of the social order – servants, tenant farmers and farm labourers – are only occasionally visible and hardly ever audible. The nearest approximation to rude language in Jane Austen comes during Fanny's sojourn with her family in Portsmouth, a return that she finds alienating rather than joyful. We know that from Fanny's point of view the language here is harsh, the actions violent and the domestic scene chaotic. Her gin-soaked father shouts loudly in the passage and with 'something of the oath kind he kicked away his son's portmanteau and his daughter's bandbox' (*Mansfield Park*, ch. 38). But what we hear of his speech is nothing worse than common nautical talk with most of the expletives deleted and a smattering of 'By G—'s. Most of the conversations and interactions in the noisy family are conveyed to us in reported speech – the author's measured phrases mediating the jarring notes of ugliness. It is not clear even to Fanny herself which is the worse offender – 'noise rising upon noise, bustle upon bustle' or 'the smallness of the rooms above and below, indeed and the narrowness of the passage and the staircase'. The roughest language to be heard in Portsmouth turns out, on close scrutiny, not to be so rough after all, and the kicking of the bandbox in the dark is the first and last 'violent' action. Fanny is indeed more appalled by the absence of smoothness and elegance which only affluence and security can produce. Here the language grates because it is the outward manifestation of a badly oiled household machinery. Fanny's refinement of taste and her fastidiousness are the natural outcome of her privileged upbringing. The basic issue thus turns out to be not language or refinement, but the presence or absence of money and the grace it affords.

The only other times when Jane Austen's characters are directly confronted by people who are clearly of a different class are when Harriet Smith is assailed by gypsies, and when Louisa Musgrove's accident on the Cobb at Lyme Regis attracts a crowd. Unlike similar dispossessed people in *The Mill on the Floss* half a century later, who speak to Maggie Tulliver and offer her their coarse food, the gypsies in *Emma* say nothing and are not presented as individuals. They are a collective threat ('half a dozen children headed by a stout woman and a great boy') and all they do is to beg silently; the noise that we hear is made not by the gypsies but by the genteel ladies, who scream. The fear of this wild unsettled class of poor people was undoubtedly rooted 'in the ladies' inarticulated consciousness of a social world composed of dangerous antagonistic groups'[8] who threaten the stability of the gentry. David Aers rightly censures this attitude, which Jane Austen evidently shared with her class, but to expect that she would use this opportunity to begin a radical interrogation of 'how the masses of uprooted rural people could survive within the gentry and bourgeois justice' is hardly realistic.[9] Not only Jane Austen, but fifty years later even George Eliot was similarly 'relieved' when her heroine managed to return to the fold – the safe ordered world of British gentry – after her brush with the nomadic poor. However, at the end of Maggie's adventure in *The Mill on the Floss*, George Eliot is uncomfortable enough to comment that Maggie 'had no idea that gypsies were not well supplied with groceries'.[10] Jane Austen, who obviously uses the gypsies not as real people but as shadowy presences on the fringes of society who can serve as a plot device to make the gallantry of a romantic rescue possible, is not troubled by any economic issues. This is clear from the way the gypsies appear and disappear speechlessly, like a pictorial image.

On the other occasion when the poor serve Jane Austen's fictional purpose – 'a charitable visit' by Emma and Harriet to a poor sick family – we neither hear nor see them, and from Emma's exclamation on leaving the cottage it would seem that they exist merely to make her luxuriate in her own sense of virtuous superiority:

> 'These are the sights, Harriet, to do one good, how tri-
> fling they make everything else appear! I feel now as
> if I could think of nothing but these poor creatures all
> the rest of the day; and yet who can say how soon it
> may all vanish from my mind?' (ch. 10).

In *Persuasion*, the workmen and the boatmen on the Cobb who collect around the site of Louisa's accident 'to be use-ful if wanted; at any rate to enjoy the sight of a dead young lady, nay two young ladies, for it proved twice as fine as the first report' (ch. 12) are also entirely silent. Henrietta is consigned to the care of 'some of the best looking of these people', who inspire the gentry's confidence by their better appearance rather than their better language.

Jane Austen's unwillingness to stretch the linguistic spectrum of her novel below the vulgar distortions of her own class is in line with her refusal to introduce characters from outside this circle. It is not that she never came across anyone who did not speak politely or did not own a carriage or employ two servants; the daughter of a clergyman, she had as much access to other social groups as had Emily Brontë, who was also a daughter of a clergyman and who used the Yorkshire dialect of her time with great effect. Jane Austen preferred to use a generally uniform language so as to emphasise the subtle variations in its use. Within this parameter she sets up a norm where superlatives and hyperboles are as much to be avoided as clichés, because one is the mark of self-indulgence and the other indicates laziness. 'Decorum' and 'propriety' are key words, and being able to articulate a sentence without flamboyance or artificiality becomes a crucial act revealing the social and moral worth of an individual.

In the last decade of the eighteenth century and in the early decades of the nineteenth, when Jane Austen wrote her novels, the privileging of order and control over excessive emotionalism was not an issue pertaining to language alone. This has to be seen as part of a wider social debate on sensibility – a term which had acquired a specialised meaning at this time – and was associated in a loose way with Jacobin sympathies in politics. The *Anti-Jacobin Review*, an organ of conservative opinion formed 'to combat the subversive principles of philosophy and politics' that were allegedly sweeping England after the French Revolution, played a leading role in the attempt to link Jacobinism or any kind of radicalism with an overcharged sensibility.[11]

But the radicals themselves, and eventually the Romantics, were equally critical of the false emotionalism that had characterised the poetry of sensibility and the novels of sentiment in the late eighteenth century. In this paradoxical debate the alignments were not sharply demarcated. It was not clear where a regard for the individual and genuine human feeling shaded into a mawkish self-indulgence, or where respect for rational institutions ossified into oppressive social conventions. Even if the opponents had taken clearly defined stands, it would still have been difficult neatly to pigeon-hole Jane Austen, who is notoriously elusive in her resistance to labels. Nevertheless, in her sustained emphasis on verbal precision and careful syntax, in her ability to coalesce antithetical positions in equivocal irony, and in her avoidance of sentimental prolixity, she seems to be carrying out in all her novels an implicit critique of all that was affected, superficial and irrational in the society she knew, as well as in its fictional representations.

Conclusion

'Men have had every advantage of us in telling their own story. Education has been theirs in so much higher a degree; the pen has been in their hands. I will not allow books to prove anything', says Anne Elliot with uncharacteristic adamancy in the penultimate chapter of *Persuasion*. We have seen that even when the pen was in women's hands, as had become increasingly common by Jane Austen's time, it had to conform to the norms set up by the dominant patriarchal culture, which provided the inescapable context of publication. Women's texts were thus implicitly made to endorse certain assumptions. The motif of the frail, frightened and nubile heroine who has to scuttle through a minefield of aggressive virility, illustrates two such interrelated assumptions: that woman is essentially the object of male sexual desire, and that chastity is the supreme female virtue.

This motif is repeated with endless variations by Jane Austen's predecessors and contemporaries, men and women alike – Richardson, Goldsmith, Fanny Burney, Henry Mackenzie, Elizabeth Inchbald, Amelia Opie, Susanna Rowson and many others. In novel after novel we see that, if the vulnerable heroines survive their ordeal, they find their reward in secure and profitable marriages; if not, they acquit themselves of the world's censure by dying martyrs' deaths. Jane Austen's steadfast rejection of this fictional staple is evident from her earliest stories in *Juvenilia*, where she repeatedly made fun of the victim heroine, to her last unfinished novel, *Sanditon*, where Charlotte Heywood picked up a copy of Fanny Burney's *Camilla* (subtitled 'A Picture of Youth') only to put it down

again because 'she had not Camilla's youth and had no
intention of having her distress' (ch. 6).

Another unspoken assumption was that a woman's prim-
ary function in life was to please men; her worth was to
be measured by her ability to attract them. The following
conversation between Emma Watson and the handsome
young Lord Osborne in *The Watsons* provides one of the
many examples in Jane Austen of the quiet subversion
of this prevalent belief. Referring to the difficulties of walking on muddy roads, Osborne says,

> 'Ladies should ride in dirty weather. Do you ride?'
> 'No, my Lord.'
> 'I wonder every lady does not – A woman never looks
> better than on horseback.'
> 'But every woman may not have the inclination, or
> the means.'[1]

Emma's response gently undermines not only the basic
male view of the world which so many women writers of
her time had unquestioningly internalised, but also the
arrogance of class and money. From Lord Osborne's van-
tage point women seemed objects of delight, entitled to
chivalric male protection if they succeeded in their attempt
to please. This attitude was no longer limited to the aristocracy. In the middle class, which was emerging as a major
force in England by the end of the eighteenth century,
women had long ceased to be actively involved in domestic
production. Their function in the economy was merely as
consumers, and their decorative qualities enhanced the
prestige of the men who provided for them. Social honour
was claimed through *gentility*; this and its lesser derivative
respectability 'were always heavily gendered categories'.[2]
A gentleman's claim to recognition was his self-sufficiency,
his independence signified by his ability to protect and
support his dependents. But the 'analogous ideal of *lady*

placed women in a protected environment away from independent action'.[3] Hence the existence and eventual acquisition of indirect power. If Jane Austen chafed against these approved codes of feminine conduct, her resistance was expressed not through any rhetoric of radical dissent, but through the witty rejoinders of her heroines and tongue-in-cheek authorial observations.

Even while mocking some aspects of the dominant ideology of her time, Jane Austen did seem to subscribe to others. For example, her central characters are all marriageable young women poised at the transition between the freedom of childhood and the subservience of wifehood. By focusing on this brief time-span in the female life cycle, she corroborates the contemporary view that a wedding is the most climactic event in a woman's life. At the same time, by exposing the economic anxiety that underlies the romantic veneer of the courtship ritual, she also achieves a partial ironic reversal.

These internal tensions inform her attitude to class also. The reprehensible Mr Elliot, heir of Kellynch Hall, can almost be forgiven for marrying for money, but not for marrying beneath his rank. Revealing his dark past Mrs Smith tells Anne, 'When one lives in this world, a man or a woman's marrying for money is too common to strike one as it ought.' Anne Elliot inquires,

> 'But was she not a very low woman?'
> 'Yes; which I objected to, but he would not regard. Money, money was all he wanted. Her father was a grazier, her grandfather was a butcher, but that was all nothing. ... Not a difficulty or a scruple was there on his side with respect to her birth.'
>
> (*Persuasion*, ch. 21)

Men who disregard class distinctions often tend also to be mercenaries in Jane Austen's novels, one vice impercep-

tibly shading into another so that it is difficult for the reader
to single out one for condemnation. This indeterminacy
works to her advantage, opening out her texts to a wider
range of sympathies.

Such strategies of indirection and accommodation apply
to her handling of the current literary conventions also,
some of which she manipulates to suit her purpose, while
she directs her irony at others. The enigma of her continuing popularity may be explained by her ability to engage
in these opposed enterprises simultaneously.

In the passage quoted at the beginning of this chapter
Anne Elliot is accusing men of holding the pen (read
'power'). But we also perceive that in another part of the
room Captain Wentworth has lost possession of his pen
by this time: 'a slight noise called the attention to Captain
Wentworth's hitherto perfectly quiet division of the room.
. . . It was nothing more than that his pen had fallen down'
(ch. 23). This reversal idirectly prepares us for Anne's
decision to take the initiative herself, thus turning upside
down the traditional gender pattern of pursuit. Finding
Wentworth unable to take a stand, Anne resolves to make
her feelings known to him. Yet it remains a characteristi-
cally ambivalent Austenian situation, because, while on
the level of praxis Anne transgresses the feminine code
of non-action, on the verbal level she keeps arguing about
the essential passivity of women's situation. She tells Captain Harville, 'All the privilege I claim for my own self
(it is not a very enviable one: you need not covet it), is
that of living longest, when existence or when hope is
gone'. Women are trapped in a situation that encourages
introspection, Anne explains: 'We live at home, quiet, confined, and our feelings prey upon us. You are forced on
exertion. You have always a profession, pursuits, business
of some sort or other to take you back into the world
immediately.'

This exchange between Captain Harville and Anne

Elliot is possibly the only overt gender debate in Jane Austen's work. Expressed gently in a rhetoric of sad resignation, Anne's views on the fate of women would have been acceptable to even the most conservative of Jane Austen's readers. This innocuousness helps the author to gain legitimacy for the unconventional act that Anne is simultaneously performing. Yet she is not being hypocritical. This is just one example of how Jane Austen can manage to contain opposite sets of impulses in the same text without negating the validity of either. In this sense she remains the quintessential novelist, because, as Milan Kundera reminds us, writing a novel is basically an ironic art: 'its truth is concealed, undeclared, undeclarable'. According to Kundera, irony not only mocks or attacks but also 'denies us our certainties by unmasking the world as an ambiguity'.[4]

This ironic ability to accommodate apparently irreconcilable values makes Jane Austen's understated and cryptic texts available to an indefinite variety and range of readings. For interpreters of fiction Jane Austen's novels seem to exert an extraordinary magnetic power. No serious critic of the English novel has been able to bypass her work, and the impressive roster of names includes Henry James, Virginia Woolf, E. M. Forster, F. R. Leavis, Edmund Wilson, Lionel Trilling, Arnold Kettle, Ian Watt, Raymond Williams, Wayne C. Booth, Barbara Hardy, Robert Scholes, David Lodge, Marilyn Butler, Tony Tanner, Susan Gubar, Sandra Gilbert and Nina Auerbach, who have provided diverse and contradictory interpretations of her novels, turning her sometimes into an orthodox apologist of Tory ideology and social hierarchy, and at others into a radical destabiliser of the status quo.

The cogency and transparency of her six completed novels obviously pose a challenge that the critic feels compelled to take up in the effort to understand the relationship between life and its fictional representation. The

growing awareness that Jane Austen does not always
encode pleasing and permanent truths in stable fictional
constructs, but allows ambiguity to operate through her
comic vision as well as through the silences and gaps in
her narrative, has in recent years made her novels a rich
site for productive new interpretations. The novelist is one
who according to Flaubert seeks to disappear behind the
work. Jane Austen thus seems the paradigmatic novelist,
both in her invisibility and in her refusal to provide us
a consistent and permanent meaning. 'The novel is the
imaginary paradise of individuals. It is the territory where
no one possesses the truth, neither Anna nor Karenin,
but where everyone has the right to be understood, both
Anna and Karenin.'[2]

To read her novels as entirely realistic and unequivocal
records of the life she knew is wilfully to overlook the
different kinds of tension in her work that the present study
has attempted to explore: between subversive parodic strategies and mimetic representations of life; between stasis
and spatial enclosure on the one hand and mobility and
expansion on the other; between the private domain of
emotion and imagination, and the public arena of propriety
and property; between a woman's need to define her individual self and society's demand that she should conform
to the familial and gender mould; between liberal sympathy and anti-Jacobin orthodoxy. Jane Austen's persis-
tently non-polemical stand and her ideological reticence
open out the novels to a range of equivocal meanings,
while her sure syntax, concise dialogue and perfectly synch-
ronised formal structures point towards a univocal certainty, baffling the critic who must coax a coherent system
out of these elusive texts. Each novel presents a different
situation, and each heroine is in a unique predicament.
If social and geographical mobility is seen as a positive
value in *Persuasion*, *Emma* reconfirms class boundaries
and spatial enclosure. If *Northanger Abbey* delights us by

its irreverence towards convention and authority, *Mansfield Park* can be read as a solemn endorsement of the hierarchical order and its code of propriety. *Pride and Prejudice* sparkles with Elizabeth's spontaneity and wit, but *Sense and Sensibility* privileges restraint and sobriety over all other qualities.

Yet these novels have enough in common to tempt the critic to try and arrive at a consistent interpretation. Even when literary meanings cannot be definitively recovered once and for all, and the stability and determinacy of the texts seem more and more uncertain, each new interpretation extends the possibilities of the text. As we have seen in the last decade or so, even though Jane Austen cannot be reconstituted as an entirely feminist writer, the fruitful feminist readings of her novels continue to enrich and enlarge our response to her novels.

Appendix:

'Plan of a Novel, According to Hints from Various Quarters'

The text of this appendix is taken from *'Plan of a Novel, According to Hints from Various Quarters' by Jane Austen, with Opinions on 'Mansfield Park' and 'Emma' Collected and Transcribed by her and Other Documents Printed from the Originals*, published in a limited edition by the Clarendon Press, Oxford, in 1926. The notes indicate the source of each 'hint'.

Scene to be in the Country, Heroine the Daughter of a [1]Clergyman, one who after having lived much in the World had retired from it, & settled in a Curacy, with a very small fortune of his own. – He, the most excellent Man that can be imagined, perfect in Character, Temper & Manners – without the smallest drawback or peculiarity to prevent his being the most delightful companion to his Daughter from one year's end to the other. – Heroine a [2]faultless Character herself – , perfectly good, with much tenderness & setiment, & not the least [3]Wit – very highly [4]accomplished, understanding modern Languages & (generally speaking) everything that the most accomplished young Women learn, but particularly excelling in Music – her favourite pursuit – & playing equally well on the Piano Forte & Harp – & singing in the first

---

[1]Mr Gifford.   [2]Fanny Knight.   [3]Mary Cooke.   [4]Fanny K.

stile. Her Person, quite beautiful – [5]dark eyes & plump
cheeks. – Book to open with the description of Father
& Daughter – who are to converse in long speeches, elegant
Language – & a tone of high, serious sentiment. – The
Father to be induced, at his Daughter's earnest request,
to relate to her the past events of his Life. This Narrative
will reach through the greatest part of the 1st vol. – as
besides all the circumstances of his attachment to her
Mother & their Marriage, it will comprehend his going
to sea as [6]Chaplain to a distinguished Naval Character
about the Court, his going afterwards to Court himself,
which introduced him to a great variety of Characters &
involved him in many interesting situations, concluding
with his opinion of the Benefits to result from Tythes being
done away, & his having buried his own Mother (Heroine's
lamented Grandmother) in consequence of the High Priest
of the Parish in which she died, refusing to pay her Remains
the respect due to them. The Father to be of a very literary
turn, an Enthusiast in Literature, nobody's Enemy but his
own – at the same time most zealous in the discharge of
his Pastoral Duties, the model of an [7]exemplary Parish
Priest. – The heroine's friendship to be sought after by
a young Woman in the same Neighbourhood, of [8]Talents
& Shrewdness, with light eyes & a fair skin, but having
a considerable degree of Wit, Heroine shall shrink from
the acquaintance. – From this outset, the Story will pro-
ceed, & contain a striking variety of adventures. Heroine
& her Father never above a [9]fortnight together in one
place, *he* being driven from his Curacy by the vile arts
of some totally unprincipled & heart-less young Man, desperately in love with the Heroine, & pursuing her with
unrelenting passion – no sooner settled in one Country
of Europe than they are necessitated to quit it & retire

[6]Mr Clarke.
[7]Mr Sherer.   [8]Mary Cooke.   [9]Many Critics.

to another – always making new acquaintance, & always obliged to leave them. – This will of course exhibit a wide variety of Characters – but there will be no mixture; the scene will be for ever shifting from one Set of People to another – but all the [10]Good will be unexceptionable in every respect – and there will be no foibles or weaknesses but with the Wicked, who will be completely depraved & infamous, hardly a resemblance of Humanity left in them. – Early in her career, in the progress of her first removals, Heroine must meet with the Hero – all[11] perfection of course – & only prevented from paying his addresses to her, by some excess of refinement. – Wherever she goes, somebody falls in love with her, & she receives repeated offers of Marriage – which she always refers wholly to her Father, exceedingly angry that[12] *he* sh^d not be first applied to. – Often carried away by the anti-hero, but rescued either by her Father or the Hero – often reduced to support herself & her Father by her Talents & work for her Bread; – continually cheated & defrauded of her hire, worn down to a Skeleton, & now & then starved to death – . At last, hunted out of civilized Society, denied the poor Shelter of the humblest Cottage, they are compelled to retreat into Kamschatka where the poor Father, quite worn down, finding his end approaching, throws himself on the Ground, & after 4 or 5 hours of tender advice & parental Admonition to his miserable Child, expires in a fine burst of Literary Enthusiasm, intermingled with Invectives again⟨st⟩ Holder's of Tythes. – Heroine inconsolable for some time – but afterwards crawls back towards her former Country – having at least 20 narrow escapes of falling into the hands of Anti-hero – & at last in the very nick of time, turning a corner to avoid him, runs into the arms of the Hero himself, who having just shaken off the scruples which fetter'd him before, was at the very

[10]Mary Cooke. [11]Fanny Knight. [12]Mrs Pearse of Chilton-Lodge.

moment setting off in pursuit of her. – The Tenderest &
completest Eclaircissement takes place, & they are happily
united. – Throughout the whole work, Heroine to be in
the most[13] elegant Society & living in high style. The name
of the work *not* to be[14] *Emma* – but of the same sort as[15]
S & S. and P & P.

[13]Fanny Knight. [14]Mrs Craven. [15]Mr H. Sanford.

Notes

Place of publication is London unless otherwise indicated.

Chapter 1.   'Gentlemen read better books'

1. John Tinnon Taylor, *Early Opposition to the English Novel* (New York, 1943) p. v, quoted in Terry Lovell, *Consuming Fiction* (London, 1987) p. 9.

2. Jean-Jacques Rousseau, *Emilius: or An Essay on Education*, tr. from the French (translator's name not given) (1763) II, 177.

3. Quoted in Catherine Macaulay Graham, *Letters on Education with Observations on Religious and Metaphysical Subjects* (1790) p. 209.

4. Hannah More, *Essays on Various Subjects Principally Designed for Young Ladies* (1778); see pp. 6 and 11.

5. Ibid., pp. 3–4.

6. Jane West, *Letters to a Young Lady, in which the Duties and Character of Women are Considered* (1806) p. 25.

7. Claudia Johnson, '"A Sweet Face as White as Death": Jane Austen and the Politics of Female Sensibility', *Novel*, 22, no. 2 (Winter 1989) 159–74.

8. Janet Todd, *Sensibility: An Introduction* (1986) p. 80.

9. Rousseau, *Emilius*, II, 177.

10. Macaulay Graham, *Letters*, p. 215.

11. Mary Wollstonecraft, *Vindication of the Rights of Woman*, ed. Carol H. Poston (New York and London, 1975) p. 29. A new analysis of Wollstonecraft can be found in Meena Alexander, *Women in Romanticism* (1990).

12. *Love and Friendship*, letter 14, in Jane Austen, *Minor Works*, ed. R. W. Chapman (Oxford, 1954).

13. Ian Watt, *The Rise of the Novel* (1957) p. 168.

14. Macaulay Graham, *Letters*, p. 48.

15. Wollstonecraft, *Vindication*, p. 29.

16. Hannah More, *Strictures on the Modern System of Female Education*, 2 vols (1799).

17. These two biographies are Henry Thomas Austen, 'Biographical Notice of the Author' prefixed to the first edition of *Northanger Abbey* and *Persuasion* (1818); and J. E. Austen-Leigh, *A Memoir of Jane Austen* (1871).

18. Austen-Leigh, *Memoir*, reproduced in the Penguin edition (1965) of *Persuasion*; see pp. 337, 330, 338.

19. *The Nation and Athenæum*, 5 Oct 1929; repr. in *Virginia Woolf: Women and Writing*, ed. Michele Barrett (New York and London, 1979) p. 97.

20. Lloyd Brown, 'Jane Austen and the Feminist Tradition', *Nineteenth Century Fiction*, 28 (1973) 321–39.

21. Margaret Kirkham, *Jane Austen, Feminism and Fiction* (Brighton, 1983) pp. 48–50.

22. A particularly amusing reference to 'Henry's History of England' in a letter to Martha written on 12 November 1800 lists in an exasperated manner the seven chapter headings in the book, 'So that for every evening in the week there will be a different subject. The Friday's lot – Commerce, Coins and Shipping – you will find the least entertaining; but the next evening's portion / Manners / will make amends.' Quoted in Austen-Leigh, *Memoir*, Penguin edn, pp. 316–17.

23. Amelia Opie, *Father and Daughter: A Tale, in Prose* (1800; 5th edn 1806) p. 190.

24. Ibid., p. 191.

25. Elizabeth Inchbald, *Everyone Has His Fault. A Comedy in Five Acts* (Dublin, 1793).

26. More, *Strictures*, pp. 48–9.

27. Judy Simons, *Fanny Burney* (1987), p. 109.

28. West, *Letters to a Young Lady*, p. 18.

29. Wollstonecraft, *Vindication*, p. 17.

30. '"I begin now to understand you all, except Miss Price," said Miss Crawford .... "Pray, is she out or is she not? I am puzzled. She dined at the Parsonage with the rest of you, which seemed like being *out*; yet she says so little, that I can hardly suppose she *is*."

'Edmund, to whom this was chiefly addressed, replied, "I believe I know what you mean, but I will not undertake to answer the question. My cousin is grown up. She has the age and sense of a woman, but the outs and not outs are beyond me"' (*Mansfield Park*, ch. 5).

31. More, *Essays on Various Subjects*, p. 34.

32. Ibid., p. 37.

33. More, *Strictures*. p. 183.

34. Wollstonecraft, *Vindication*, p. 184.

35. Reproduced in appendix II of Frank W. Bradbrook, *Jane Austen and her Predecessors* (Cambridge, 1966) p. 145.

36. Quoted in Joyce Henlow, 'Fanny Burney and the Courtesy Books', *PMLA*, 65, no. 5 (Sep 1950) 740.

37. Hannah More, *Coeleb in Search of a Wife* (1808) I, 245.

38. Terry Lovell, *Consuming Fiction* (1987) p. 11.

39. More, *Strictures*, p. 32.

40. Judy Simson, *Fanny Burney* (1987) p. 8.

41. Quoted in Bradbrook, *Jane Austen and her Predecessors*, pp. 114–15.

42. Maria Edgeworth, Preface to *Belinda* (1801).

43. See the title-page of Amelia Opie, *Father and Daughter*.

44. Simson, *Fanny Burney*, p. 14.

45. William Empson, *Some Versions of the Pastoral* (1933) p. 62.

Chapter 2.   'But you know, we must marry'

1. Fay Weldon, *Letters to Alice on First Reading Jane Austen* (1984) p. 27.

2. Fanny Burney, *Evelina* (1778).

3. Letter written on 20 February 1817; quoted in John Halperin, *The Life of Jane Austen* (1984), p. 322.

4. Weldon, *Letters to Alice*, p. 30.

5. Letter quoted in Halperin, *Life of Jane Austen*, p. 310.

6. Ibid.

7. The chronology of Mary Shelley's life at this period is as follows:

    1815   girl child born premature; dies in a few days
    1816   a son, William, born
    1817   a daughter, Clara, born
    1818   Clara dies
    1819   William dies
    1819   a son, Percy Florence, born

This information is provided in Mary Shelley, *Frankenstein*, ed. James Kinsey and M. K. Joseph (Oxford, 1969).

8. Elizabeth Gaskell, *The Life of Charlotte Brontë* (1857) p. 27.

9. Charlotte Smith, *D'Arcy: A Novel* (Dublin, 1793) p. 36.

10. This phrase appears in W. H. Auden's poem 'Letter to Lord Byron' (1936), where he admires Jane Austen's clear-eyed view of money and marriage:

> It makes me most uncomfortable to see
> An English spinster of the middle class
> Describe the amorous effects of 'brass',
> Reveal so frankly and with such sobriety
> The economic basis of society.

11. More, *Essays on Various Subjects*, p. 133.

12. Christopher Gillie, *A Preface to Jane Austen* (1974) p. 10.

13. Gaskell, *Life of Charlotte Brontë*, pp. 46–7.

14. As set down at length in More, *Essays on Various Subjects*.

15. Halperin, *Life of Jane Austen*, p. 280.

16. Letter quoted ibid., p. 266.

17. Kirkham, *Jane Austen*, pp. 66–73.

18. *The Adventurer*, no. 115 (11 Dec 1753).

19. This letter written in 1837 was originally inserted 'in Mr C. C. Southey's life of his Father vol. VI, p. 327'. Elizabeth Gaskell cites the source while quoting it in *Life of Charlotte Brontë*, p. 109.

20. Ibid., p. 104.

21. Mary Poovey, *The Proper Lady and the Woman Writer: Ideology as Style in the Works of Mary Wollstonecraft, Mary Shelley and Jane Austen* (Chicago: University of Chicago Press, 1984).

Chapter 3. 'To hear my uncle talk of the West Indies'

1. Amelia Opie, *Father and Daughter*, p. 90.

2. Charlotte Smith, *D'Arcy*, p. 150.

3. Jane Austen, *Shorter Works*, Folio Society edn (1963) p. 179.

4. See for example Austen-Leigh, *Memoir*, Penguin edn, p. 277; Halperin, *Life of Jane Austen*, pp. 19, 53; Park Honan, *Jane Austen: Her Life* (1987) p. 43.

5. Halperin, *Life of Jane Austen*, p. 19. Park Honan says, 'Possibly

Warren Hastings took Mr Austen's sister as his mistress' (*Jane Austen: Her Life*, p. 43).

6. Austen-Leigh, *Memoir*, Penguin edn, p. 43.

7. Ibid., p. 290.

8. Halperin, *Life of Jane Austen*, p. 62.

9. Ibid., p. 207.

10. James Boswell, *Journal of a Tour to the Hebrides*, ed. Allan Wendt (Boston, Mass., 1985) p. 250.

11. Quoted in Halperin, *Life of Jane Austen*, p. 257.

12. David Aers, Jonathan Cook and David Punter, *Romanticism and Ideology: Studies in English Writing, 1765–1830* (1981) pp. 128–9.

13. Jane Austen wrote about this book, 'I expected nothing better. Never did any book carry more internal evidence of its author. Every sentence is completely Egerton's' (quoted in Halperin, *Life of Jane Austen*, p. 81).

14. Raymond Williams, *The English Novel from Dickens to Lawrence* (1973) p. 19.

Chapter 4.   'Crowd in a little room'

1. Tony Tanner, *Jane Austen* (1985) p. 190.

Chapter 5.   'Admiring Pope no more than is proper'

1. Umberto Eco, *The Name of the Rose*, Picador edn (1984) p. 286.

2. Lovell, *Consuming Fiction*, p. 53.

3. Sheridan's *The Rivals* (1775) gives an amusing and concise account not only of the reading-material that was popular among young girls at the time, but also of what was considered approved reading:

>   LYDIA. Here, my dear Lucy, hide these books. Quick, quick. – Fling *Peregrine Pickle* under the toilet – throw Roderick Random into the closet – put *Innocent Adultery* into *The Whole Duty of Man*, thrust Lord Ainsworth under the sopha – cram Ovid behind the bolster – there – out – *The Man of Feeling* into your pocket – so, so, now lay Mrs Chapone in sight and leave Fordyce's *Sermons* open on the table.
>   LUCY. O burn it, Ma'am, the hairdresser has torn away as far as *Proper Pride*.
>   LYDIA. Never mind – open at *Sobriety*. Fling me Lord Chesterfield's *Letters*. Now for 'em.   (I.ii)

4. Letter written in 1798, quoted in Halperin, *Life of Jane Austen*, p. 82.

5. Elaine Showalter, *A Literature of their Own* (Princeton, NJ, 1977).

6. Tanner, *Jane Austen*, p. 45.

7. As paraphrased by Ian Watt in *The Rise of the Novel*, Penguin edn (1963) p. 174.

8. Kirkham, *Jane Austen*, p. 97.

9. Samuel Taylor Coleridge, *Biographia Literaria*, ed. J. Shawcross (Oxford, 1969) ii, 182. Discussing Lessing's dramatic works, Coleridge writes, 'their deficiency is in depth and imagination; their excellence is in the construction of the plot; the good sense of the sentiments; the sobriety of the morals; and the high polish of the diction and dialogue. In short his dramas are the very antipodes of all those which it has been the fashion of late years to abuse and enjoy under the name of German drama.'

Chapter 6. 'Speak well enough to be unintelligible'

1. Jane Austen's letter to her niece Anna, quoted in Halperin, *Life of Jane Austen*, p. 26.

2. As Oliver Goldsmith did in *Chinese Letters*, subsequently republished as *Citizen of the World* (1762).

3. Virginia Woolf, *A Room of One's Own* (1929), Penguin edn (Harmondsworth, 1974), p. 155.

4. More, *Coeleb in Search of a Wife*, p. 245.

5. Todd, *Sensibility*, p. 125.

6. Tony Tanner points out, 'More than one critic has suggested that Mary Crawford, with her quick wit, her vitality, and resilience is more like Jane Austen herself than the shrinking Fanny' (*Jane Austen*, p. 154).

7. Nina Auerbach, 'Jane Austen's Dangerous Charm', in Janet Todd (ed.), *Jane Austen: New Perspectives* (1983) p. 219.

8. Aers, in Aers, Cook and Punter, *Romanticism and Ideology*, p. 131.

9. Ibid.

10. George Eliot, *The Mill on the Floss* (1860), Signet Classics edn (1965) p. 123.

11. *The Oxford Companion to English Literature* (Oxford, 1960) p. 30.

12. Todd, *Sensibility*, p. 143.

Conclusion

1. *Lady Susan / The Watsons / Sanditon*, ed. Margaret Drabble (Harmondsworth, 1974) p. 178.

2. Leonore Davidoff, 'The Role of Gender in the First Industrial Nation: Agriculture in England 1780–1850' in Rosemary Crompton and Michael Mann, *Gender and Stratification* (Cambridge, 1986) p. 191.

3. Ibid.

4. Milan Kundera, *The Art of the Novel*, tr. Linda Asher (1988).

Bibliography

Selected Critical Studies

Abel, Elizabeth, Marianne Hirsch and Elizabeth Langland (eds), *The Voyage In: Fictions of Female Development* (University Press of New England, 1983).

Aers, David, Jonathan Cook and David Punter, *Romanticism and Ideology: Studies in English Writing 1765–1830*, essays on Blake, Wordsworth, Coleridge, Jane Austen, Shelley and Hazlitt (London: Routledge and Kegan Paul, 1981).

Argess, Lynne, *The Feminine Irony: Women on Women in Early Nineteenth Century English Literature* (Hanover, NH, and London: Associated University Presses, 1978).

Auerbach, Nina, 'O Brave New World: Evolution and Revolution in *Persuasion*', *ELH*, 39 (1972) 112–28.

Babb, Howard S., *Jane Austen's Novels: The Fabric of Dialogue* (Ohio University Press, 1963).

Barfoot, C. F., *The Thread of Connection: Aspects of Fate in the Novels of Jane Austen and Others* (Amsterdam: Rodepi, 1982).

Beer, Patricia, 'What Became of Jane Austen', *TLS*, 25 July 1982.

Berger, Carole, 'The Rake and the Reader in Jane Austen's Novels', *Studies in English Literature*, 15, no. 4, 531–44.

Bradbrook, Frank W., *Jane Austen and her Predecessors* (Cambridge: Cambridge University Press, 1968).

——, 'Style and Judgement in Jane Austen's Novels', *Cambridge Journal*, June 1951.

Brown, Julia Prewitt, *Jane Austen's Novels: Social Change and Literary Form* (Cambridge, Mass.: Harvard University Press, 1979).

Brown, Lloyd, *Bits of Ivory: Narrative Techniques in Jane Austen's Fiction* (Baton Rouge, Louisiana State University Press, 1973).

——, 'Jane Austen and the Feminist Tradition', *Nineteenth Century Fiction*, 28 (1973) 321–38.

Browne, Alice, *The Eighteenth Century Feminist Mind* (Brighton: Harvester Press, 1987).

Brownstein, Rachel M., *Becoming a Heroine: Reading About Women in Novels* (New York: Viking, 1982).

Bush, Douglas, *Jane Austen* (London: Macmillan, 1975).

Butler, Marilyn, *Jane Austen and the War of Ideas* (London: Oxford University Press, 1975).

——, *Romantics, Rebels and Reactionaries: English Literature and its Background (1760–1830)* (Oxford: Oxford University Press, 1982).

Chapman, R. W., *Jane Austen: Facts and Problems* (London: Oxford University Press, 1948).

Drew, Philip, 'Jane Austen and Bishop Butler', *Nineteenth Century Fiction*, 35 (1980) 127–49.

Duckworth, Alistair H., *The Improvement of the Estate: A Study of Jane Austen's Novels* (Baltimore: John Hopkins University Press, 1971).

Eagleton, Mary, and David Pierce, *Attitudes to Class in the English Novel from Walter Scott to David Storey* (London: Thames and Hudson, 1979).

Elsbree, Langdon, 'Jane Austen and the Dance of Fidelity and Complaissance', *Nineteenth Century Fiction*, 15 (1960).

Fergus, Jan, *Jane Austen and the Didactic Novel* (New York: Barnes and Noble, 1983).

Figes, Eva, *Sex and Subterfuge: Women Writers to 1850* (London: Macmillan, 1982).

Fleishman, Avron, *A Reading of 'Mansfield Park': An*

Essay in Critical Synthesis (Minneapolis: University of Minnesota Press, 1967).

——, 'The State of the Art – Recent Jane Austen Criticism', *Modern Language Quarterly*, 37, no. 3, 281–9.

Gilbert, Sandra and Susan Gubar, *The Madwoman in the Attic: Nineteenth Century Literary Imagination* (New Haven, Conn.: Yale University Press, 1979).

Gillie, Christopher, *A Preface to Jane Austen* (London: Longman, 1974).

Gooneratne, Yasmine, *Jane Austen* (Cambridge: Cambridge University Press, 1970).

Greene, D. J., 'Jane Austen and the Peerage', *PMLA*, 68 (1953) 1017–31.

Gubar, Susan, 'Sane Jane and the Critics', *Novel*, 8, no. 3, 246–59.

Halperin, John, *Jane Austen: Bicentenary Essays* (Cambridge: Cambridge University Press, 1975).

——, *The Life of Jane Austen* (Brighton: Harvester, 1984).

Harding, D. W., 'Regulated Hatred: An Aspect of the Work of Jane Austen', *Scrutiny*, 1940.

Hardy, Barbara, *A Reading of Jane Austen* (London: Peter Owen, 1975).

Hardy, John, *Jane Austen's Heroines: Intimacy in Human Relationships* (London: Routledge and Kegan Paul, 1984).

Hart, Francis, 'The Spaces of Privacy: Jane Austen', *Nineteenth Century Fiction*, 30 (1975) 305–33.

Hemlow, Joyce, 'Fanny Burney and the Courtesy Books' *PMLA*, 65, no. 5 (Sep 1950).

Hogan, Charles Beecher, 'Jane Austen and her Early Public', *Review of English Studies* (1950) 39–54.

Honan, Park, *Jane Austen: Her Life* (London: Weidenfeld and Nicolson, 1987).

Hough, Graham, 'Narrative and Dialogue in Jane Austen', *Critical Quarterly*, 1970.

Kaplan, Deborah, 'Achieving Authority: Jane Austen's

First Published Novel', *Nineteenth Century Fiction*, 37 (1983) 531–51.

Kelley, Grace, *The English Jacobin Novel, 1780–1805* (Oxford: Clarendon Press, 1976).

Kincaid-Weeks, Mark, 'The Old Maid: Jane Austen Replies to Charlotte Brontë and D. H. Lawrence', *Nineteenth Century Fiction*, 31 (1976) 188–205.

Lane, Maggie, *Jane Austen's England* (London: Robert Hale, 1986).

Lascelles, Mary, *Jane Austen and her Art* (London: Oxford University Press, 1939).

Laski, Marghanita, *Jane Austen and her World* (New York: Viking, 1969, 1975).

Leavis, F. R., *The Great Tradition* (London: Chatto and Windus, 1948).

Leavis, Q. D., 'A Critical Theory of Jane Austen's Writings', *Scrutiny*, x (June and Oct 1941, Jan 1942).

Lenta, Margaret, 'Jane Austen's Feminism', *Critical Inquiry*, 23 (1981) 27–35.

Levine, George, 'Translating the Monstrous: *Northanger Abbey*', *Nineteenth Century Fiction*, 30 (1975) 335–50.

Lewis, C. S., 'A Note on Jane Austen', *Essays in Criticism*, 1954.

Litz, A. Walton, *Jane Austen: A Study of her Artistic Development* (London: Chatto and Windus, 1965).

——, 'Recollecting Jane Austen', *Critical Inquiry*, 1, 669–82.

Lovell, Terry, *Consuming Fiction*, Questions for Feminism series (London: Verso, 1987).

Luria, Gina (ed.), *The Feminist Controversy in England 1788–1810* (New York: Garland, 1974).

Mahl, Mary R., and Helen Koon (eds), *The Female Spectator: English Women Writers before 1800* (New York: Feminist Press, 1977).

Mansel, Darrel, *The Novels of Jane Austen* (New York: Barnes and Noble, 1973).

McMaster, Juliet (ed.), *Jane Austen's Achievements* (London: Macmillan, 1976).

Mews, Hazel, *Frail Vessels: Woman's Role in Women's Novels from Fanny Burney to George Eliot* (London: Athlone Press, 1969).

Miller, D. A., *Narrative and its Discontents: Problems of Closure in the Traditional Novel* (Princeton, NJ: Princeton University Press, 1981).

Miller, Jane, *Women Writing about Men* (London: Virago, 1986).

Monaghan David (ed.), *Jane Austen in a Social Context* (London: Macmillan, 1981).

——, *Jane Austen: Structure and Social Vision* (London: Macmillan, 1980).

Moler, Kenneth L., *Jane Austen's Art of Allusion* (Lincoln, Nebr.: University of Nebraska Press, 1968).

Moore, Margaret, 'Emma and Miss Bates', *Studies in English Literature*, 9 (1969) 573–85.

Morgan, Susan, *In the Meantime: Character and Perception in Jane Austen's Fiction* (Chicago: University of Chicago Press, 1980).

——, 'Polite Lies: The Veiled Heroine of Sense and Sensibility', *Nineteenth Century Fiction*, 31 (1976) 188–205.

Mudrick, Marvin, *Jane Austen: Irony as Defense and Discovery* (Princeton, NJ: Princeton University Press, 1952).

Myers, Sylvia H., 'Womanhood in Jane Austen's Novels', *Novel*, 3 (1970) 225–32.

Nardin, Jane, *Those Elegant Decorums: The Concept of Propriety in Jane Austen's Novels* (Albany, NJ: State University of New York Press, 1973).

Odmark, John, *An Understanding of Jane Austen's Novels: Character, Value and Ironic Perspective* (Oxford: Basil Blackwell, 1981).

Piggott, Patrick, *The Innocent Diversion: A Study of Music in the Life and Writings of Jane Austen* (London: Douglas Cleverdon, 1979).

Pinion, F. B., *A Jane Austen Companion: A Critical Survey and Reference Book* (London: Macmillan, 1975).

Poovey, Mary, *The Proper Lady and the Woman Writer: Ideology as Style in the Works of Mary Wollstonecraft, Mary Shelley and Jane Austen* (Chicago: University of Chicago Press, 1984).

Roberts, Warren, *Jane Austen and the French Revolution* (London: Macmillan, 1979).

Rees, Joan, *Jane Austen: Woman and Writer* (London and New York: St Martin's Press, 1976).

Scholes, Robert, 'Dr Johnson and Jane Austen', *Philological Quarterly*, 54, no. 1, 380–90.

Schorer, Mark, 'Pride Unprejudiced', *Kenyon Review*, 18 (Winter 1956).

Schott, P. J. M., *Jane Austen: A Reassessment* (London: Vision Press, 1982).

Simons, Judy, *Fanny Burney*, Women Writers series (London: Macmillan, 1987).

Smith, LeRoy W., *Jane Austen and the Drama of Women* (London: Macmillan, 1983).

Spencer, Jane, *The Rise of the Woman Novelist, from Aphra Behn to Jane Austen* (Oxford: Basil Blackwell, 1986).

Springer, Marlene, *What Manner of Woman* (New York: New York University Press, 1977).

Southam, B. C. (ed.), *Critical Essays on Jane Austen* (London: Routledge and Kegan Paul, 1968).

Stone, Donald D., 'Sense and Semantics in Jane Austen', *Nineteenth Century Fiction*, 25 (1970).

Tanner, Tony, *Jane Austen* (London: Macmillan, 1986).

Tave, Stuart M., *Some Words of Jane Austen* (Chicago: University of Chicago Press, 1973).

Ten Harmsel, Henrietta, *Jane Austen: A Study in Fictional Conventions* (The Hague: Mouton, 1964).

Todd, Janet, *Women's Friendship in Literature* (New York: Columbia University Press, 1980).

——, *Feminist Literary History* (Cambridge: Polity Press, 1988).

——, (ed.), *Be Good, Sweet Maid: An Anthology of Women and Literature* (New York: Holms and Heier, 1981).

——, (ed.), *Jane Austen: New Perspectives*, special issue of *Women and Literature* (New York: Holms and Heier, 1983).

Tomalin, Claire, *The Life and Death of Mary Wollstonecraft* (London: Weidenfeld and Nicolson, 1974).

Tompkins, J. M. S., 'Elinor and Marianne: A Note on Jane Austen', *Review of English Studies*, XVI.

Tucker, George Holbert, *A Goodly Heritage: A History of Jane Austen's Family* (Manchester: Carcanet, 1983).

Wardle, Ralph M., *Mary Wollstonecraft: A Critical Biography* (Lawrence: University of Kansas Press, 1951).

Watt, Ian (ed.), *Jane Austen: A Collection of Critical Essays*, Twentieth Century View series (Englewood Cliffs, NJ: Prentice-Hall, 1963).

Weinsheimer, Joel (ed.), *Jane Austen Today* (Athens, Ga: University of Georgia Press, 1975).

Weissman, Judith, 'Evil and Blunders: Human Nature in *Mansfield Park* and *Emma*', *Women and Literature*, 4, no. 1 (Spring 1976) 5–17.

Weldon, Fay, *Letters to Alice on First Reading Jane Austen* (London: Michael Joseph, 1984).

Wilson, Mona, *Jane Austen and Some Contemporaries* (London: Hogarth, 1938).

Woolf Virginia, *The Common Reader* (London: Hogarth, 1925).

——, *Women and Writing*, ed. Michele Barrett (New York and London: Harcourt Brace, 1979).

Books by Jane Austen's Contemporaries and Predecessors: A Selected List

Burney, Frances, *Evelina* (1778), ed. Edward Bloom (London: Oxford University Press, 1968).

——, *Cecilia* (1782; London: Virago, 1986).

——, *Camilla or A Picture of Youth* (1796), ed. Edward and Lilian Bloom (Oxford: Oxford University Press, 1983).

——, *The Wanderer or Female Difficulties* (London: Longman, 1814).

Edgeworth, Maria, *Belinda* (London: J. Johnson, 1802).

Fordyce, James, *Sermons to Young Women*, 4th edn, 2 vols (London: A. Millar and T. Cadell, 1776).

Godwin, William, *Memoirs of Mary Wollstonecraft* (1798), ed. Clark Durant (London: Constable, 1927).

Gregory, Dr John, *A Father's Legacy to his Daughters* (London and Edinburgh: Strahan Cadell and Creech, 1788).

Inchbald, Elizabeth, *A Simple Story* (1791), ed. J. M. S. Tompkins (London: Oxford University Press, 1967).

Kotzebue, August Friedrich Ferdinand von, *Das Kind der Liebe*, tr. from the German as *Lovers' Vows* by Mrs Inchbald, 4th edn (London: G. C. and J. Robinson, 1798).

Macaulay, Catherine, *An Address to the People of England, Scotland and Ireland, on the Present Important Crisis of Affairs*, 2nd edn (London: E. and C. Dilly, 1775).

——, *Letters on Education with Observations on Religious and Metaphysical Subjects* (1790), ed. Gina Luria (New York: Garland, 1974).

——, *Observations on the Reflections of the Right Hon. Edmund Burke, on the Revolution in France* (Boston, Mass.: I. Thomas and E. T. Andrews, 1791).

More, Hannah, *Essays on Various Subjects, Principally*

Designed for Young Ladies (London: T. Cadell and W. Davies, 1778).

——, *Strictures on the Modern System of Female Education*, 2nd edn, 2 vols (London: T. Cadell and W. Davies, 1799).

——, *Coeleb in Search of a Wife*, 2 vols (London: T. Cadell and W. Davies, 1808).

Opie, Amelia, *Father and Daughter: A Tale in Prose* (1800), 6th edn (London: Longman, 1806).

Rousseau, Jean-Jacques, *Emilius or an Essay on Education*, tr. from the French by Mr Nugent (London: J. Nourse and P. Valliant, 1763).

Radcliff, Ann, *The Romance of the Forest* (London: T. Hookham and J. Carpenter, 1791).

——, *The Mysteries of Udolpho, A Romance; Interspersed with Some Pieces of Poetry* (London: G. G. and J. Robinson, 1794).

——, *The Italian, or the Confessionals of the Black Penitents, A Romance*, 2nd edn, 3 vols (London: T. Cadell, 1797).

Smith, Charlotte, *Celestina: A Novel* (London: T. Cadell, 1791).

——, *D'Arcy: A Novel* (Dublin: P. Wogan, 1793).

West, Jane, *Letters to a Young Lady in which the Duties and Character of Women are Considered* (1806), ed. Gina Luria (New York: Garland, 1970).

Wollstonecraft, Mary, *Thoughts on the Education of Daughters* (1787; Clifton: Augustus Kelley, 1972).

——, *Mary and the Wrongs of Woman*, ed. Gary Kelly (Oxford: Oxford University Press, 1983). This edition contains *Mary, A Fiction* (1788) and *Maria or the Wrongs of Woman* (1798).

——, *A Vindication of the Rights of Men, in a Letter to the Right Honourable Edmund Burke Occasioned by his Reflections on the Revolution in France* (London: Joseph Johnson, 1790).

——, *Original Stories from Real Life with Conversations Calculated to Regulate the Affections and Form the Mind* (London: Joseph Johnson, 1791).

——, *A Vindication of the Rights of Woman* (1792), ed. Carol Poston (New York: Norton, 1975).

Index

Aers, David, 64, 151
Anti-Jacobin Review, 134
Astell, Mary, 13
Auden, W. H., 150
Auerbach, Nina, 137
Austen, Henry Thomas, 11, 51
Austen, Jane,
  Emma, 26, 43, 48, 56, 60,
    61, 62, 63, 64, 65, 67,
    68, 69, 73, 74, 78, 82,
    83, 86, 114, 127, 128,
    132, 141
  Juvenelia, 50, 136
  Letters, 31, 33, 43
  Love and Friendship, 8
  Mansfield Park, 18, 35, 37,
    42, 48, 51, 53, 54, 55,
    56, 59, 61, 62, 65, 70,
    71, 72, 73, 78, 102, 104,
    105, 106, 108, 112, 121,
    129, 130, 131, 142
  Northanger Abbey, 8, 23,
    24, 31, 41, 60, 61, 66,
    72, 93, 94, 97, 98, 100,
    101, 102, 106, 116, 117,
    118, 130, 141
  Persuasion, 9, 18, 39, 40, 42,
    48, 56, 57, 58, 60, 63,
    66, 67, 68, 69, 71, 72,
    75, 76, 79, 82, 83, 86,
    101, 105, 114, 115, 133,
    136, 137, 141
  Plan of a Novel, 24, 25, 26,
    143
  Pride and Prejudice, 3, 9,
    18, 19, 22, 31, 35, 37,
    40, 41, 45, 47, 48, 54,
    58, 61, 65, 66, 72, 74,
    75, 76, 77, 78, 81, 82,
    92, 95, 101, 111, 114,
    118, 122, 131, 142
  Sanditon, 23, 38, 39, 81, 90,
    101, 104, 136
  Sense and Sensibility, 9, 31,
    32, 36, 38, 41, 48, 51,
    52, 61, 66, 71, 72, 76,
    77, 81, 82, 91, 95, 98,
    103, 110, 111, 113, 114,
    126, 127, 128, 130, 142
  The Watsons, 35, 44, 78, 137
Austen-Leigh, J. E., 11, 148

Beckford, William,
  The Elegant Enthusiast, 90
Bhagavad-Gita, 54
Booth, Wayne C., 140
Boswell, James, 151
Bradbrook, Frank, 13
Brontë, Charlotte, 34, 44, 46,
  121
  Jane Eyre, 44, 60, 78
  Villette, 78
Brown, Lloyd, 13
Browning, Elizabeth Barrett,
  47
  Aurora Leigh, 47
Brydges, Samuel Egerton,
  Fitzalbini, 66
Burney, Fanny, 2, 10, 22, 23,
  24, 30, 93, 136
  Camilla, 14, 136
  Evelina, 1, 10, 24, 25, 30

The Wanderer, 17
Butler, Marilyn, 12, 140

Chapone, Mrs, 51
Chesterfield, Earl of, 4
Coleridge, Samuel Taylor, 3
  Biographia Literaria, 106, 152
  'Kubla Khan', 54
Cowper, William, 1, 102, 103
Crabbe, George, 1, 102
Crosby, 45

Defoe, Daniel, 29, 59
Dickens, Charles
  David Copperfield, 59
  Hard Times, 59

Eco, Umberto,
  The Name of the Rose, 89
Edgeworth, Maria, 2, 23, 93
  Belinda, 23
Elegant Extracts, 92
Eliot, George, 34, 133
  Adam Bede, 59
  Middlemarch, 40, 78
  The Mill on the Floss, 78, 132, 133
Empson, William, 24

Flaubert, Gustave, 141
Fordyce, Revd. James, 5
  Sermons to Young Women, 23
Forster, E. M., 140

Gaskell, Elizabeth, 34, 150
Gilbert, Sandra, 12, 137
Gillie, Christopher, 150
Godwin, William, 11, 13, 15
Goldsmith, Oliver, 9, 50, 136
  Citizen of the World, 53

The Vicar of Wakefield, 6, 92
Gregory, Dr John, 5
Gubar, Susan, 12, 137
Gulliver's Travels, 53

Halperin, John, 33, 51
  Letters of a Hindoo Rajah, 53
Harding, D. W., 12
Hardy, Barbara, 12, 137
Hastings, Warren, 51, 54
Henry VIII, 104
Holcroft, Thomas, 15

Idler, The, 102
Inchbald, Elizabeth, 2, 11, 13, 15, 107, 136, 148
  Everyone Has His Fault, 15
  A Simple Story, 15, 24, 25
  Wives as They Were and Maids as They Are, 16

James, Henry, 137
  The Portrait of a Lady, 40, 47, 85
Johnson, Claudia, 6, 147
Johnson, Samuel, 2, 46, 54
Jones, William, 54

Kettle, Arnold, 140
Kirkham, Margaret, 12, 13, 45, 106, 148
Kotzbue, August von, 107
  The Lover's Vows (Das Kind der Liebe), 107, 108, 109
Kundera, Milan, 140, 153

Lascelles, Mary, 12
Lawrence, James, 53
  The Empire of the Nairs, 53
Leavis, F. R., 140

Lennox, Charlotte, 90
    The Female Quixote, 90
Locke, John, 3
Lodge, David, 140
Lovell, Terry, 21, 147
Lover's Vows, The, 55, 104,
        105, 106, 107, 108, 109,
        129

Macaulay, Catherine Graham,
        7, 10, 11, 147
Mackenzie, Henry, 136
Monthly, 2
Moore, Edward,
    Fables of the Female Sex, 21
Moore, Thomas,
    Lalla Rookh, 45, 54
More, Hannah, 4, 5, 11, 16,
        17, 20, 43, 44, 147, 148,
        149
    Coeleb in Search of a Wife,
        21, 123
Mudrick, Marvin, 12
Mysteries of Udolpho, The,
        120

Opie, Amelia, 2, 11, 13, 15,
        23, 136, 148
    Father and Daughter, 14, 15,
        23, 25, 50, 148
Opie, John, 14
Owenson, Sydney, Lady
        Morgan, 93
    Ida Athens, 93
    *The Missionary, an Indian
        Tale*, 54
    The Wild Irish Girl, 93

Pasley, Captain Sir Charles,
    *Essay on the Military Policy
        and Institutions of the
        British Empire*, 52
Pennington, Lady Sarah, 20

*An Unfortunate Mother's
        Advice to Her Absent
        Daughters*, 20
Poovey, Mary, 47, 150

Radcliffe, Ann, 121
Rambler, The, 98
Reeve, Clara,
    The Progress of Romance,
        22
Richardson, Samuel, 1, 6, 9,
        93, 102, 136
    Charissa, 6
    Pamela, 20, 21, 42, 59
    Sir Charles Grandison, 102
Roche, Regina Maria,
    Children of the Abbey, 92
Rousseau, Jean-Jacques, 2, 7,
        13, 147
    Emilius, 7, 147
Rowson, Susanna, 136

Sales, Roger, 64
Scholes, Robert, 137
Scott, Sir Walter, 3, 103
    Marmion, 45
Shelley, Mary, 34, 149
Shelley, Percy Bysshe,
    Prometheus Unbound, 54
Sheridan,
    The Rivals, 23, 151
Showalter, Elaine, 96
Smith, Charlotte, 13
    D'Arcy, 25, 38, 50
Southey, Robert, 46, 54
    The Curse of Kehama, 54
Sterne, Laurence, 29
Syke, Mrs,
    *Margianna, or Widdington
        Towers*, 93

Tanner, Tony, 108, 140, 152

Thackeray, W. M.,
    Vanity Fair, 40, 60
Todd, Janet, 6, 12, 147, 152
Tompkins, J. M. S., 25
Trilling, Lionel, 137
Trollope, Anthony, 28

Utopia, 53

Villette, 78

Watt, Ian, 10, 21, 140
Weldon, Fay, 149
West, Jane, 5, 17, 147

Williams, Raymond, 140, 151
Wilberforce, 55
Wilson, Edmund, 140
Wollstonecraft, Mary, 2, 7, 8,
    10, 11, 13, 16, 17, 18, 20,
    22, 45, 147
    *Vindication of the Rights of
        Women*, 7, 10, 13, 15,
        18
    Wrongs of Women, 14, 15
Woman and Literature, 12
Woolf, Virginia, 13, 34, 121,
    140, 148
Wordsworth, William, 3
Wuthering Heights, 78

Thackeray, W. M.
Tomlinson, H. M.
Todd, Janet 142, 147, 152
Tompkins, J. M. S. 65
Trilling, Lionel 15n
Trollope, Anthony 25

Jungian 87

Villette 76

Well, Ian 103, 110
Wopkins, 110
Warehouse, S. H. 79

Williams, Raymond 103, 137
Wilberforce 55
Wilson, Edmund, 140
Wollstonecraft, Mary 2, 3,
10, 13-15, 16, 21, 35, 36,
43, 45, 147
Womanhood, the Right of
Women 10, 1, 15

Rights of Women 13, 152
Woman and Literature 13
Woolley, Hannah 43, 54, 121
130, 148
Wordsworth, William
Wuthering Heights 75